Old-Fashioned Fun and Games

E. O. Harbin

BAKER BOOK HOUSE
Grand Rapids, Michigan

Formerly published under the title:
Phunology

Paperback edition issued 1978
by Baker Book House
with permission of copyright owner

ISBN: 0-8010-4184-8

Library of Congress Catalog
Card Number 53-5395

CONTENTS

MONTHLY PROGRAMS

CONTENTS

MONTHLY PROGRAMS

MONTHLY PROGRAMS

CHAPTER I

JANUARY PROGRAMS

SEASON SOCIAL

A season social would go well in January. Divide the company into four groups, Winter, Summer, Autumn, and Spring, according to the month of birth of each one. Thus December, January, and February would form the winter group, and so on.

Decorate booths or rooms appropriately as headquarters for the various groups. For instance, Winter could decorate in white or could use the red and green color scheme, with holly and cedar to help the appearance. Summer could use potted plants to advantage. Hanging birds or butterflies would also add to its "summery" appearance. Autumn could decorate with autumn leaves, real or imitation, or it might use the Halloween idea, with jack-o'-lanterns, witches, black cats, and yellow and black crêpe paper. Spring could achieve a Maypole table, using pink and white crêpe paper streamers with small dolls at the outer edges of the table holding the streamers, or artificial daisies could be used in profusion.

Let the groups now engage in contests of various sorts. Have each prepare some stunt or give a yell or sing a song.

The following contests can be used: The Standing Broad Smile, the Baby Marathon, the Banana Feed, and the Cracker Relay, all of which appear elsewhere in this book.

This social can be adapted to any time of the year if desired.

Decorations and Refreshments

Decorations

Summer.—Flags and national colors.

Winter.—White color scheme. Sprinkle with diamond dust. Use a sleigh as a centerpiece. Touch off the white with a bit of holly and red.

Spring.—Green and white, with plenty of natural or artificial flowers.

Autumn.—Brown and red, with autumn leaves and chrysanthemums.

Refreshments

Summer.—Lemonade and cakes tied with red, white, and blue ribbons.

Winter.—Ice cream and frosted cake.

Spring.—Lettuce sandwiches and olives.

Autumn.—Fruit.

Another Season Social

Decorations

Spring.—Green and pink crêpe paper. Potted plants. Spring may be spelled with green and pink paper flowers on some sort of cloth for background.

Summer.—Lots of greenery. Japanese lanterns. Flowers.

Autumn.—Autumn leaves and Halloween decorations.

Winter.—Color scheme—white. Use plenty of cotton batting. Sprinkle with diamond dust. One group spelled winter in large cotton letters using heavy string to form the background or frame for the letters.

Plan

The crowd is divided into four groups according to the season in which they happen to be born. Each of these appoints a leader and practices yells and songs. Each group is responsible for managing one of the events as described in this article. Judges should be appointed to determine winners in the various contests. The score-keeper should post the scores on the blackboard as they are made.

Events

1. *Yelling Contest.*—If desired judges may require the four groups to give yells or sing a song and award points for first, second, and third places.

2. *Snowball Contest.*—This contest is conducted by Winter at its booth. A hoop one foot or so in diameter which has been covered with white and three contestants from each group (preferably girls) line up about ten feet from the hoop. They are provided with three snowballs of loose cotton batting. Each contestant gets three throws. The ball going through the hoop scores one point for the team and the team with the highest score is awarded first place. This contest is entirely managed by the Winter group.

3. *Spring Fever Race.*—About ten contestants for each team, more or less is desired. A pillow is given each team. At a signal to start the first person on the team pulls the pillow out of its casing and then puts it back in. After

doing this he passes it on to the next team mate who goes through the same performance. This is continued on down the line until the last player on the team has gone through the necessary performance and rushes to the head of the line holding the encased pillow aloft and calling out the name of his side. Spring, of course, is responsible for managing this new event. It should be seen that all pillows and casings are the same size so no one team will have an advantage.

4. (*a*) *Honeymoon Race.*—Boy and girl to represent each group. Each couple is provided with a suitcase in which is wearing apparel of all sorts. A hat, kimono, pair of men's shoes for the girl and a hat, raincoat for the boy. Each couple is also provided with an umbrella. All suitcases are shut and strapped. At a signal to go couples arm in arm rush to one end of the room open suitcases and don wearing apparel. The boy then opens the umbrella, closes the suitcase with the girl's own shoes inside and arm in arm they rush back to the starting point. Here they must take off wearing apparel, put it back in suitcase. The girl must put on her own shoes; the umbrella must be shut. The first couple to finish, of course, wins.

(*b*) *Fanning Bee.*—One contestant from each group. Each contestant is given a palm leaf fan and a toy balloon. At a signal to start contestant must bat the toy balloon up in the air and then keep it in the air until they have reached the goal at the other end of the room. If it is allowed to hit the ground the contestant must pick it up with the fan. He is not allowed to roll it along the floor.

Both of these contests are managed by the Summer group.

5. *Football Tournament.*—Two tables about four feet in length should be provided. These tables should be covered with green or brown wrapping paper which should be drawn tightly over the surface. This wrapping paper then

should be marked off with chalk to represent a football field. Goal posts should be set up at both ends of the field. These goal posts could be easily made by setting up standards about six inches high in half spools. A cross-bar should be tacked to these standards. The distance between these posts should be about eight inches. Eleven players from each team line up at either end of the field. One at a time they blow the football attempting to send it through the opponent's goal. The ball is of course placed in the center of the field after each attempt. The football is an egg that has been emptied of its contents by punching a small hole in either end of the egg and blowing out the contents. This can be dropped in a coffee pot and browned or it can be painted with water colors. With pen and ink make the lacing and seams so as to make it look like a football. Several extra footballs had better be on hand for emergency. If the football goes through the opponent's goal post it counts a touch-down and six points. If it goes the goal line but not through the goal post it counts two points. The last quarter of the game may be played by having both teams have all their players blow at once. In this case the goal posts are removed and the touch-down is scored when the ball goes over or touches the goal line. In this quarter the referee places the ball in the center of the field. The player starts blowing when he sounds his whistle. If the ball goes outside it is brought back into the field at the point at which it went outside, just as it would be in a regular football game. No player is allowed to put his face over in the field. If he does his side is penalized for off side play.

Winter can play Summer and Spring can play Fall at the same time.

The winners would then play a final game to determine the football champion.

This contest is managed by the Autumn group.

In the scoring five points should be allowed for first place, three points for second, and one point for third. The score should be recorded on a blackboard so everybody can see the standing of the groups.

A NEW YEAR'S JAMBOREE

Your invitation might read as follows:

JAMBOREE! OUI! OUI!
In what month were you born!
You needn't confess,
But wear something that tells
So that we may guess.

To make yourself at home
We want you to feel free
Next Thursday night at eight
At our New Year's Jamboree.

(Name of organization, place and date)

Urge every one to come wearing something representative of the month of his birth. You might require those who disregard your request to pay a fine.

January could wear a very small naked doll labeled "19——," or could come dressed as a snow man or snow girl.

February could wear a white dress covered with red paper hearts or wear a cherry or small toy hatchet on the lapel of the coat, or a miniature picture of Washington would do.

March might wear a shamrock, a bit of green ribbon, or a toy clay pipe. A pair of bellows might be carried and used frequently to remind folks that in March the winds do blow.

April could be arrayed in raincoat and carry an umbrella. A dunce cap or jester's cap and bells might be used. A piece of foolscap paper worn on the dress might keep them guessing.

May could wear a rose tied to a small American flag, indicating Decoration Day, or a crown on the head and chains of flowers hung about the neck would indicate that the "May Queen" was in attendance.

June could come as a bride or in cap and gown as a sweet girl graduate. A rose worn in the lapel of the coat or in the hair or a corsage bouquet of roses would indicate the month of roses.

July might shine forth in patriotic colors. A Columbia costume would be fitting. An American flag could be worn. Some clever boy might make up as an animate firecracker. A large cylindrical hatbox, or two of them put together, covered with red paper, a piece of rope glued to the top for a fuse, eyeholes cut out so that the "firecracker" might see where to walk, the whole thing slipped over the head and shoulders of the boy, and the thing is done.

August could come as a girl or boy in summer attire carrying a tennis racket. Or some one might think of it as the month of Tennyson's birth and come with a copy of "Sweet and Low" or "In Memoriam" pinned on him. King Arthur and his Knights of the Round Table might also think of coming to the party.

September could come arrayed in overalls or wear a toy spade, indicative of Labor Day. Schoolbooks would indicate it as the month school begins.

October could wear some Halloween novelty—witch, pumpkin head, black cat, etc. A dress covered with autumn leaves (these could be made out of paper if the real leaves are not available) would do very well. "The one-hundred-per-cent American" pinned on the lapel of the coat might remind some one that this is the month of Theodore Roosevelt's birth.

November would be easy. A picture of a turkey, a

miniature football worn on the dress or coat, a Camp Fire girl carrying a basket or fruit, a football player—any of these would do.

December could wear a sprig of holly or a picture of Santa Claus. Some one might come dressed as Santa. A clever costume of red and green with trimmings of holly might be conceived.

These and many more ingenious ways to represent the month of their birth will be thought of by the young people.

The first thing on the program would be the guessing of the birth month of each one present. The names and months should be written on a sheet of paper by each guest. A souvenir calendar is given to the person giving the most correct answers.

Now the crowd indulges in stunts for each month of the year.

Snowball Battle

For January a snowball battle could be staged. The crowd would be divided into two sides. A ball of cotton batting is given to the leader of each side. The idea is to throw this ball through a suspended holly wreath. Each player in turn has one try, a point being scored when the "snowball" goes through the wreath. Captains should line up their players and see that there is no delay in having the players take their turns.

Heart Hunt

February announces a hunt for paper hearts, awarding some prize for the one who finds the most.

Grand March

March will start a grand march about the room in which everybody takes part, the leader winding in and out, trotting or walking as the mood may strike him, finishing by winding the party about in a spiral march, reversing his direction when he reaches the center and unwinding the spiral as the grand climax.

Peanut Hunt

April announces a peanut hunt; and after the crowd has scrambled about awhile in vain search, the leader informs them it is an "April fool."

Spring Song

Some one could play Mendelssohn's "Spring Song" as a piano solo for May, or some rollicking ring game, such as "Farmers in the Dell," could be played for a few minutes.

Dress the Bride

For June provide each one with a clothespin, some white crêpe paper and string, and ask them to dress the bride. Allow five minutes for this.

"Firecrackers"

For July pass out "firecrackers" which are sticks of candy wrapped in red tissue paper with a string fuse at the top.

"Jography"

September might divide the guests into four groups according to the seasons. Then conduct a rapid-fire geography quiz after this manner: The leader calls for the name of either a city, river, or mountain, and then announces the letter with which it must begin. For instance, the leader shouts "City—B." The Autumn group, perhaps, shouts "Boston" just before Spring gets out "Baltimore."

Score one for Autumn. Ten calls will be enough. The group with the highest number of points could then be announced as winner.

Fortunes

Have fortunes written on slips of paper. Place these in two boxes, one for boys and one for girls. Let each one draw a fortune.

"A Yell-'m-Up"

For November ask each of the groups for September to get up an appropriate yell. Or the game of table foot-ball might be played, with representatives of the groups as contestants. This game is described in Chapter XI.

"Eats" and Santa

For August let the refreshments be served picnic fashion, Santa Claus representing December superintending the distribution of the "eats."

"Pep" Hint

The person in charge of the program should see that everything is run off in rapid order. Have no delays or hitches. Wise planning will be required. To borrow a camp expression, you must "make it snappy."

A CALENDAR SOCIAL

Invitations might be written on a card, with a page from a small calendar pad pasted in one corner.

Stunts

As persons arrive have each write on a slip of paper his name and the month of his birth. No one is to see what is written except the committee in charge. This committee assorts the slips by months and then calls out names of persons in each group, asking them to get together and prepare a stunt representative of their month. Allow from fifteen minutes to a half hour for this. The rest of the crowd guesses the name of the month and shouts it out as soon as some one guesses correctly.

January could stage a snowball fight with handkerchiefs or have a scene in which the old year departs and the new year enters.

February could celebrate a few birthdays—Washington, Lincoln, or Longfellow, for instance. A burlesque on the cutting down of the cherry tree might be worked out. A clever mock trial could be arranged in which Dan Cupid is arraigned for having wrought havoc in the local society.

March folks could storm or march about. All of them could talk at once and incessantly. Surely somebody would guess that people so "windy" must represent March.

April could have a cornet solo which continues after the cornet has been taken from the lips of the player, a concealed victrola furnishing the music. A violin solo may also be played in the same manner.

May could put on a Maypole dance.

June could have a wedding.

July could celebrate the Fourth or could reproduce some patriotic scene.

August might have a picnic, playing some rousing games and sitting about on the floor and eating an imaginary picnic dinner.

September could have opening day at school.

October could pull off some Halloween pranks. It could make some local hits by having a fortune teller answer imaginary questions for some of those present. A ghost story might be told.

November might stage an imaginary football game, lining

up, calling signals, and pretending to run with the ball. Or the Novemberites could do a lot of "Rah-rah-ing," having a yell leader to direct them. Or they might have a mimic Thanksgiving feast, after which they might feign Thanksgiving stomach aches.

December could be represented by the singing of "Silent Night, Holy Night" or other Christmas songs. Or it might be represented by children that are painfully good.

Good Resolutions

Now each person is given paper and pencil and asked to write "Resolved" at the top. Underneath this each is to write six New-Year resolutions, serious or otherwise. If the crowd is large, three resolutions will be plenty. These are collected, and some one reads them. The rest try to guess the authorship of each set of resolutions.

Next the guests are asked to write a New-Year resolution for some one else in the crowd. As each of these is read, guesses are made as to the person for whom the resolution was written.

Calendar Basket Ball

Now suspend twelve baskets, each with the name of a month on it. Provide twelve rubber balls, each with the name of a month printed on it in black. The trick is to see who can place the greatest number of balls in the right baskets. The score does not count if the ball does not go into the basket of the same name. Each person is allowed two throws with each ball. The baskets may be put on the floor in a row and the players be required to toss from a line several feet away from the first basket, much after the fashion of the old game of "Soakey." Award a calendar as a prize to the most proficient player.

Calendar Race

If another game is needed, you might try a calendar race. Have the crowd divided and lined up on two sides. Give the leader of each line a set of twelve cards on which are written the names of the months. These cards are mixed up before being given to the leaders. At the signal to go these leaders start the cards down their respective lines one at a time. The end player as he receives the cards puts them on the floor at his feet. When he has received all twelve cards and arranged them in proper order—January, February, March, etc.—he proceeds to pick them up and start them back down the line. The first side whose leader receives all twelve cards and arranges them properly on the floor wins the race.

On the plate with the refreshments have a date to which is fastened with a toothpick a card or piece of paper bearing this query: "Will you make a *date* to meet with the ——— Sunday evening at 6:30?"

A TWELFTH-NIGHT CAKE PARTY

The 6th of January is Twelfth-night, or Old Christmas. In the olden days the Yuletide festivities continued for a period of twelve days, which was the time supposed to be consumed by the three wise men in their journey to Bethlehem. Thus the season of gayety culminated on the evening of January 6, or Twelfth-night. In England and on the Continent it used to be the occasion for elaborate social functions. A ring was concealed in an immense cake, and the guest obtaining it was made "king" or "queen." Every vestige of Christmas green was supposed to be taken down and burned. This was a peace offering to evil spirits and insured good luck to the household.

Cakes are to Twelfth-night what the tree is to Christmas. In London, so one writer tells us, on the night before this festival there are always crowds before the bakery shop windows to see the wonderful display of cakes of all sorts and sizes, some of them ornamented in all sorts of ingenious ways. With this in mind, a cake party is decidedly apropos.

Ask each girl to come in costume representing a cake, cooky, or doughnut, and each boy to come attired as a baker.

Each cake may come accompanied by a baker, or some sort of mixing game may be used after the crowd assembles, and thus each girl will get a baker for a partner.

There are all sorts of possibilities in costume creations.

A dress trimmed with a fringe of tiny sponges would represented *sponge cake.*

A dress of alternate brown and white ruffles and a chocolate drop cap, *chocolate cake.*

A white dress adorned with little red devils and a little devil figure in the hair will represent *devil cake.*

Cup cake could be represented by some one wearing a fringe of tin cups.

Bride's cake, by a bridal costume.

Marble cake, by one dressed in a gown with layers of white, pink, and brown.

Angel food, by white costume with wings.

Pictures of hens sewed on the dress could represent *layer cake.*

Martha Washington cake, by some one in colonial costume.

Oatmeal cake, by some one with Quaker oats signs sewed over the dress.

Ribbon cake, a white dress with spangles of ribbon.

A Cake-Guessing Contest

1. The society woman's cake? Reception.
2. The schoolgirl's? Composition.
3. The profiteer's? Sugar.
4. The parasite's? Sponge.
5. The lazy man's? Loaf.
6. The minister's? Scripture.
7. The milliner's? Feather.
8. The old lady's favorite? Tea.
9. The milkman's? Cream.
10. The sculptor's? Marble.
11. William Jennings Bryan's favorite? Silver.
12. Suitable for your lady love? Angel.
13. A favorite with most girls? Wedding.
14. The politician's delight? Plum.
15. The candidate for office? Election.
16. The prize fighter's cake? Pound.
17. The gossip's cake? Spice.
18. The champion track team? Cup.
19. The lover's cake? Kisses.
20. The baby's cake? Pat-a-cake.
21. The ball player's? Battercake.
22. Those who indulge too freely in these? Stomach ache.

An additional list of cakes that may be suggested for the costumers might include pancake, battercake (young man in baseball uniform and carrying a bat), fruit cake, orange cake, cooky, coffee, etc.

A cake might be baked in which are hidden a bean, a pea, and a clove. The guest getting the bean becomes king, the one getting the pea becomes queen, and the one getting the clove becomes court jester. Should these go to the wrong sex, the persons getting them may choose whom they will have to serve. Crowns should be provided for the king and queen and a jester's cap or dunce cap for the court jester. The game of "King and Queen" as described in the February chapter may be used.

Let the king with appropriate ceremony decorate the winner in the cake contest with a pasteboard "medal," while the queen places a wreath of some sort on the champion's head. The court jester can perform the same sort of ceremony for the winner of the booby prize, pinning on the medal and then decorating the "boob" with a dunce cap.

Refreshments, cake and hot chocolate.

JUMPING THE CANDLES

A stunt that could be tried at a New Year's social is the old stunt of jumping the candles. Twelve lighted candles are placed upright on the floor, numbered from one to twelve. One at a time the players jump over them from side to side. The candle snuffed out in this manner indicates the month in which the person will marry. If no candle is snuffed out, it indicates that the person will not be married during the year.

WRITING RESOLUTIONS WITH LETTERS

Give out a list of ten letters and have every one write a New Year's resolution, using the letters in the order in which they were given out.

CHAPTER II

FEBRUARY PROGRAMS

A LEAP YEAR PARTY

Every four years comes leap year, when February lays claim to twenty-nine days and the young ladies are privileged to "pop the question." A merry party could be arranged combining the leap year with your Valentine party.

Your invitation, with place and date, might feature this bit of rhyme:

"One year in four
We girls adore,

For this is leap year time.
So watch your step;
They'll get you yet
As some one's valentine.
Now get the date
And don't be late.
We want you to help us celebrate."

In a crowd where all are well acquainted it would be lots of fun to have the girls go for the boys and escort them to the party.

The girls should take the initiative in every way, helping the men off with their coats, seeing that they are comfortably seated, holding doors open for them, and paying them all the little courtesies usually shown to ladies by well-bred gentlemen.

Pulling Heartstrings

Suspend from the chandelier or in the doorway two large hearts made of red paper and hung several inches apart. Make a hole in each, through which are run red strings of considerable length, the ends hanging down on either side. The men take hold of the strings on one side and the girls on the other, everybody being careful not to draw the strings taut. At the signal all pull their strings, the hearts are riven, and partners are found holding the ends of the same string. This gives the couples for the next game.

Progressive Confab

Each person has been provided with ten small hearts cut out of red paper. They sit in a circle about the room in couples and are given a subject on which to converse for two minutes. The use of any personal pronoun in the conversation is barred. The person disobeying this rule must surrender one of the paper hearts to the person with whom he or she is conversing for each infraction. At the end of the two minutes each girl rises and moves to the next man, the men remaining seated. A new topic is given out, and this is continued until a certain number of subjects have been discussed. Some subjects that may be used are: "Childhood Days," "School Days," "First Sweethearts," "Friendship," "Love," "Marriage," "Old Agė," etc.

WINK

Keeping the partners with whom they find themselves at the close of the Progressive Confab, the company can now indulge in the old game of "Wink," with the girls doing the winking. Each girl will step behind the chair of her partner. An odd player will have to be used to stand behind an empty chair. She winks at one of the men, and he must endeavor to elude his guard and go to the winker's chair. The girl guarding may not step from behind her chair, but most endeavor to hold him in the chair. The girl losing her partner becomes winker, and the game continues.

PROGRESSIVE PROPOSALS

The men are provided with a number of small hands and mittens cut out of paper. It would help add to the merriment of the occasion if the men were provided also with fans behind which to hide their blushes. The girl does the proposing. When she is accepted, she is given a hand. If she is rejected, she "gets the mitten." At the tap of a bell each girl moves to the next man to try her luck once more. So it continues until each girl has made the rounds or, in case there is too large a crowd for this, until a certain time has elapsed. The girl who has collected the greatest number of hands in this time could be awarded some suitable prize. A consolation prize might also be given to the one with the greatest number of mittens.

Two More Stunts

If other games are desired, why not give out to each man a little bit of tissue paper, a needle, some thread, and a peanut and have him dress up the peanut as a doll?

Let each girl write a proposal of marriage to some real or fictitious character. These are collected by the leader and read, some award being made for the most clever proposal.

Refreshments

Each girl has been instructed to bring an apron, and now the boys don these aprons and serve the refreshments without help from the girls, who wait to be served. A plentiful supply of heart-shaped cookies has been made by the girls during the week, and these and "Love Potion" are served. "Love Potion" is our old friend lemonade, with a few oranges, some grated pineapple, and a bit of grape juice added. This makes a delightful drink.

Additional Subjects for Progressive Confab

Which does a man love best, his mother, his wife, or his sweetheart?

Which is the best way to a man's heart, through his eyes or his ears?

Whose love is truest, a man's or a woman's?

What are women's rights?

What is your ideal man or woman?

Some Other Valentine Games

Matrimony

Let the players see how many small words they can make out of the word "matrimony" in a given time, say ten minutes.

King and Queen of Hearts

Select a girl and a boy to act as King and Queen of Hearts. Have gilt paper crowns decorated, with red paper hearts for each. Improvise a throne and decorate it appropriately. The queen and the king sit side by side. Subjects approach the throne one at a time, first a girl, then a boy, and so on. Each girl goes to the king and kneels before him. He whispers instructions in her ears, handing her a large red cardboard heart. Each boy kneels before the queen. Every one must do as bidden. For instance, the queen hands the heart to a boy, who starts the game by kneeling before her, and whispers: "Give this heart to the prettiest girl in the room." The boy makes his decision after more or less deliberation, hands the heart to some girl without a word of explanation, and takes his seat. The girl now reports to the king, kneels, and hands back the heart. He returns it with instructions perhaps to give it to the boy who is "the best entertainer." Each must remember to whom he or she gave the heart and why, but is to tell no one until commanded to do so by the king and queen. At the close, when each one in the circle has had the heart at least once, the king instructs all the players to tell to whom they gave the heart and for what reason, beginning with the first player to report to the throne and then in order to the last person. It may have been for "the biggest feet" or "biggest ears" or "most beautiful eyes" or "the one who would make the most ideal wife," etc.

Heart Toss

Make two sets of heart-shaped rings of heavy wire, three to each set. Cover with ribbon or crêpe paper. Wind one stake with gilt paper to represent Wealth, hearts ringing it counting five points. The second stake may be longer than the rest and have a laurel wreath at its base. Ringing it counts ten. It represents Fame. Wind the third stake, which might be shaped like an arrow, with pink and have a circle of paper hearts above its base. This is Love, and ringing it counts twenty-five points. Each player gets a try with the tree rings, and the first one to make 500 may be declared winner. Or you could choose sides and have the side totaling the highest number of points in one time around declared victor. In this case each side would be provided with a set of rings.

A READING FOR A LEAP YEAR OR VALENTINE PARTY

Little Mary's Essay on Husbands

Husbands is the people that your Mammas marry, and she always wishes she hadn't picked out the one she did, but I don't know why, 'cause Husbands all look alike to me.

My Mamma says that husbands are like the things you buy on the Bargain Counters. They look just fine and grand, and you think you'll die if you don't get the one you got your eyes set on, and you fight other women for it, and after you get it and take it home with you and keep it awhile it looks like 30 cents, and you spend your life wondering what made you fool enough to want it.

There used to be a lot of husbands, and it was as easy to go out and get one as it was to shoot a buffalo for breakfast, but every year they got fewer and fewer; and they don't roam the Plains any more, and soon there won't be any husbands or buffaloes left 'cept those in captivity.

My Mamma says that there's no other wild animal in the world as hard to tame as a husband, and then, even after you've had hobbles on one for four or five years, it's liable to break loose and jump over the fence.

Husbands is very nice and polite to strange ladies, and they laugh themselves most to death when pretty slim young ladies tells funny stories; but when their wives are forty years old and have gotten fat, husbands is grouchy, and when their wives tells funny stories all they say is "Humph!"

Husbands is strange creatures, but all the Young Ladies is trying to catch one, and all the Old Ladies that's got double chins that shake when they talk is a-trying to keep the ones they've got.

There are two kinds of husbands, good husbands and bad husbands. Good husbands is one that gives his wife lots of money to spend and goes down town at 8 o'clock and don't come home till 6 o'clock. And a husband that's a mean old thing is one that makes his wife buy things on a bill so he can see how she spends the money, and goes snooping around the kitchen to see how thick the cook pares the potato peelings, and stays at home all day.

A husband is a right useful animal to have around the house, 'cause it pays the bills.

I'm gona have a husband when I'm grown up.—*Author unknown.*

A HEART SOCIAL

Write invitations on heart-shaped cards on which may be written these words: "Have a heart and accept our invitation to attend a Valentine heart social Monday, February 14, 8 P.M."

Decorate with hearts cut out of red paper or cardboard. Make strings of these hearts and festoon the walls, drop from chandelier, doorsill, etc.

Mixing Game

Give out hearts that have been cut in two pieces, one piece being given to a girl and another to a boy. No two hearts should be cut just exactly alike. The cut may be straight, curved, saw-toothed, through the middle, off a corner, etc. Be sure to keep them in two piles, so they will match up properly. Have girls and boys match for partners.

Heart Hunt

Now let the partners engage in a heart hunt. Have tiny red hearts, and a few gold ones perhaps, hidden about the room. Let the players hunt to some rollicking tune played on the piano. The pianist will stop playing for short intervals every now and then, and the hunters must retain whatever position they may be in when the music ceases until its starts again. If any gold hearts are used, they may count five points, the red ones counting one. The couple with the highest number of points at the close of the hunt may be given some sort of prize, such as a small heart-shaped box filled with candy.

Heart-and-Dart Game

Make a large red heart out of cardboard. Paste on it eight or ten small white paper hearts. Number these. Write on the blackboard or post in a conspicuous place the meaning of each heart. For instance, No. 1 may mean "matrimonial success," No. 2 may mean "no chance," No. 3, "domestic warfare," etc. Players may be divided into sides and the score kept to determine the winner. Each player gets one turn at throwing a dart at the big heart. Whichever small heart he hits records his score as well as his fortune. Darts may be easily made by using a feather, a cork, and a pin. A piece of paper crisscrossed in the cork makes a good substitute for the feather.

Progressive Hearts

Now play progressive hearts, tally cards having been

given each player. A set of cubes, six in number, is on each table. This game may be bought, or the cubes may be homemade. Get enough cubes of wood from some carpenter shop and mark the sides of each with the letters H-E-A-R-T-S. Each player in turn throws these out on the table. If an H turns up, it counts 5, H E counts 10, and so on. Of course if the thrower turns up two H's he is not entitled to 10, nor to 20 if he turns up two H E's. Five times around constitutes a game, and the boy and the girl with the highest score at each table progress to the next table, having tally cards punched. All players must record their own scores for each game on the tally cards. If any player turns three H's, all the score made in that game previous to that throw is canceled. At the close scores are totaled, and suitable prizes may be given to the boy and the girl with the highest scores.

Hot chocolate and heart-shaped cookies may be served for refreshments.

A CUPID PARTY

A cupid party,
A welcome hearty,
A bunch of young folks gay.
Won't that suffice?
Now be real nice
And join us in our play.
(Name of organization)
(Place)
(Date)
(Time)

The above invitation, written on white paper cut in heart shape, folded over note size, and sealed with a tiny red heart, was given out to all the young people of the Church.

Cupid Search

Cut valentines (either fancy or comic, post card, etc.) into two or three pieces. Hide the fragments about the room. The fun consists in seeing which two or three persons can soonest construct a complete valentine by searching out the players holding matching pieces which they have found in the hurried scramble. If larger groups are desired, the valentines may be cut in the number of pieces necessary. These groups when formed may be asked to put on stunts or may engage in various contests.

Cupid Pie

Each player is now given a piece of paper shaped like a pie cut, on which are written a number of words appropriate to the season, with the letters all jumbled:

1. Tahresaceh.
2. Ssseik.
3. Gsish.
4. Oevl rlestte.
5. Moprsesi.
6. Revsol larrques.
7. Sugh.
8. Lapsopro.
9. Gemtagneen gnir.
10. Rargamie larta.

Answers: 1. Heartaches. 2. Kisses. 3. Sighs. 4. Love letters. 5. Promises. 6. Lovers' quarrels. 7. Hugs. 8. Proposal. 9. Engagement ring. 10. Marriage altar.

Cupid Archery

Make a bow and arrow. A rib out of an old umbrella, with a strong piece of cord tied across the ends, will serve admirably for your bow. A long stick, with a bit of cardboard stuck in one end and a small sharpened nail or pin in the other, makes your arrow. Gild the arrow.

The target will be a large wooden or cardboard heart covered with muslin. The outside rim of the heart is red and is labeled "Acquaintance Avenue"; the next is white and is labeled "Friendship Pike"; the third is red and bears the inscription, "Lovers' Lane." The small heart in the center is "City of Love." These count, respectively, 5, 10, 15, and 20 points.

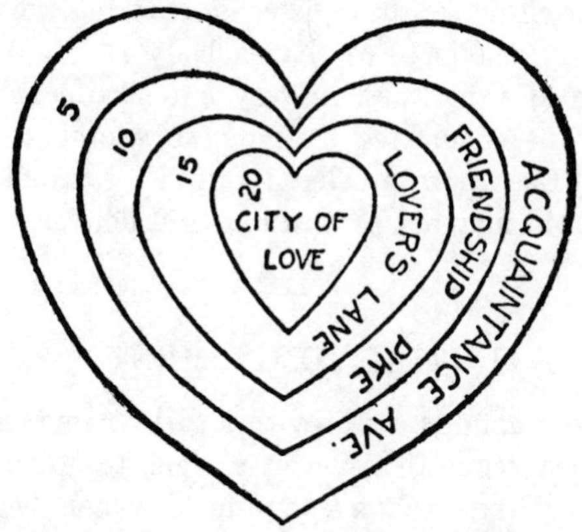

Divide the company into sides and let them contest.

Be sure to see that the walls are protected from wild shots on either side of the target.

Cupid Toss

Each of the two sides now forms a semicircle. A sandwich basket or other low basket is placed in the center, and each side, being provided with an equal number of cardboard hearts, one side with white, the other red, attempts to toss the hearts into the basket. If there are so many players as to make the circle too large, have them contest ten from each side at a time. When all players have participated, count the hearts in the baskets so as to determine whether the whites or the reds have won.

Serve "cupid punch" (lemonade with the addition of some grape juice or loganberry juice and grated pineapple) and "love caresses" (lady finger cakes).

CUPID'S POST OFFICE

Require each person to register on entering the door. In this way you can be sure that nobody is left out in the distribution of valentines. Every one should bring a few valentines, the committee having a few others for emergency use. Each person calls at Cupid's post office for his mail, or Cupid may act as postman and deliver them.

INITIAL COMPLIMENT

Each boy is handed a slip with a girl's name on it. The boys are then requested, one at a time, to go to the girls designated, giving each a compliment which begins with the initial letter of the girl's name.

As each girl is addressed by a boy she replies, using the initial letter of his first name in her answer.

HEARTS AND MITTENS

Where you desire to mix your crowd, pair them off in couples and divide them into two sides for some contest that is to follow. Nothing better can be found than this plan:

Cut out of red cardboard half as many hearts and mittens as you expect in your company. Out of blue cardboard cut the same for the rest of your party.

Number them so each heart will have a corresponding

mitten. Attach a string to each and place them in a basket, the strings hanging outside.

Each person takes hold of a string and pulls out a heart or mitten, as it may be. Each one then looks for his or her partner.

When all are paired off, a double circle is formed, and some one at the piano strikes up a lively march. Whenever the music stops, all the girls stand still, and the boys move up one. This continues until every one has had a different partner, and finally when the original one comes all indulge in a grand march before the circle breaks up. Now the reds and the blues may contest with one another in various games.

LOVE LETTERS

Players write love letters addressed to persons of opposite sex, either imaginary or chosen from present company. These are read aloud at the close of the time limit, papers having been exchanged by passing them all two players to the right. Prizes may be awarded for the two best.

BLIND DART

On a square of white muslin drawn taut upon the wall paste a large heart cut from a piece of old red velvet or plush. Players are blindfolded, given a gilded dart, and told to proceed to the heart and thrust the dart into the heart. All players succeeding may draw for a prize.

VALENTINE BUBBLES

Suspend from a portière rod between the hall and reception room or from the balcony or chandelier three hearts formed of wire and covered with crêpe paper. Above each is a jingle:

1. Blow your bubble right through here,
   And you'll be married within the year.

2. To be engaged within the week,
   Number 2 is the one you seek.

3. An awful fate for number three,
   A spinster or bachelor you will be.

Have a bowl filled with bubble solution on a table and a clay pipe and small fan for each guest. The bubbles must be first thrown off the pipe and then blown through the hearts with the fans.

VALENTINE FISHING

Cut out celluloid hearts. Punch a small hole in each one. They may bear the names of the girls present. Each young man fishes with rod, line, and pin hook for these hearts as they float on the surface of the water in a tub.

VALENTINE QUOITS

Make tiny heart-shaped wire quoits and two wooden pegs representing gilded arrows. Set these in a gilded wooden base, and players can indulge in a game of valentine quoits.

SHORT ESSAY

Let the girls write short essays on "The Ideal Man." Let the boys write short essays on "The Ideal Woman."

VALENTINE FORTUNES

Put these on a table and let the players blindfolded walk to the table and touch one of them. They indicate the fortunes of the players, as follows:

Handful of rice. Approaching marriage.

Pink cardboard stuck full of tiny hearts. Flirt.

Mitten. Rejection or (in case of girl) declination of offer of marriage.

Toy reins. This person will be driven in matrimonial harness.

Bit of crêpe. Beware of widows or widowers.

Toy cat, teapot, or thimble. Spinster, bachelor.

Pop corn. (Boy) "Propose soon, and you will be successful"; (girl) "You must be ready to help him out."

Two matches or two rings. Married twice.

Coin. You will marry wealth.

Paper snake. Beware of a rival to enter your Eden.

VALENTINE FISHPOND

A number of fishponds are laid out on a long table. These ponds are suit boxes or other large pasteboard boxes with slits cut in the bottom. Boxes are put on the table, bottom up, and valentine post cards are fitted into the slits, with just one corner showing. In this corner a hole has been punched. Each player is provided with a fishing line, a small stick with a red cord and bent pin completing the equipment. Every one fishes for valentines.

HEART ARCHERY

Heart-shaped target of wood or cardboard covered with white muslin. The outside rim is green, the next is black, the third is yellow, the fourth blue, the fifth red—all together giving the appearance of a series of hearts. Each player shoots with bow and arrow, the color upon which he hits determining his fate.

Love and riches both we deem
Fit for you who hit the green.

Should you shoot and hit the blue,
You will find a love that's true.

If you pass each blooming one,
Love for you has just begun.

If the red your dart should pierce,
The way you'll fight'll be something fierce.

Into the black,
Nary a smack.

Should you by some chance hit yellow,
Your girl'll soon have another fellow.

He whose arrow goes astray
Will surely throw his heart away.

Display these couplets on a cardboard or on the blackboard where every one can see them. Have some one remove the arrows as fast as they are shot.

VALENTINE GAME

Give ten minutes to see who can make the most words out of the letters in "valentine."

VALENTINE MISSES

1. What miss sometimes causes amusement and sometimes trouble? Mischief.

2. What miss is distrustful of human nature? Misanthrope.

3. What miss undervalues her opportunities, Misappreciate.

4. What miss is not honest? Misappropriate.

5. What miss is a blunderer? Mistake.

6. What miss can destroy the peace of a home, school, or nation? Misrule.

7. What miss wastes time and money? Misspend.

8. What miss proves an uncertain correspondent? Misdirect.

9. What miss must a traveler shun? Misguide.

10. What miss gets into court often? Misdemeanor.

11. What miss brings trouble and sorrow? Misfortune.

12. What miss shows signs of being ill bred? Misbehave.

13. What miss often twists the meaning of statements? Misconstrue.

14. What miss is untruthful? Misrepresent.

15. What miss makes the world better? Missionary.

16. What miss do we all like to receive, especially if she comes from the home town? Missive.

17. What miss is not a miss? Mister.

18. What miss comes in handy at Christmas time? Mistletoe.

19. What miss ruins business? Mismanagement.

20. What miss is an object of pity? Miserable.

21. What miss is in the wrong place? Misfit.

22. What miss loses lots of things? Mislay.

23. What miss has the wrong name? Misnomer.

24. What miss does an unpopular speaker sometimes have to dodge? Missile.

25. What miss is a woman hater? Misogynist.

SUGGESTION FOR "EATS"

It helps wonderfully to give things new names suitable to the occasion. For instance, lemonade need not be just plain lemonade, but you may call it "love potion." Lady fingers would be "love caresses," candy would be "love sweets," cakes may be "Cupid cakes" or "Cupid confections," and so on.

It would be lots of fun to serve ice cream to couples and have them eat each from his or her saucer with spoons that are tied together with a string nine inches long.

CUPID'S WHEEL OF FORTUNE

Make a wheel of fortune out of cardboard. Mark it off in twelve sections, naming these sections "journey," "success," "true love," "health," "happiness," "early marriage," "wealth," "matrimonial bliss," "domestic trouble," "single cussedness," etc. Fasten an indicator to the center of the wheel and let each player have a spin to see what Cupid's wheel has to tell him.

BROKEN-HEART PUZZLE

Supply each couple with a heavy paper or cardboard heart which has been cut in eight pieces like a jig-saw puzzle. These should all be cut alike, so that no couple will have an advantage. The first couple to put the heart together, thus mending the "broken" heart, may be given an appropriate prize.

FAMOUS LOVERS' PIE

Give out the following list of jumbled names of famous lovers:

1. Even I, angel—Evangeline.
2. Hurt—Ruth.

3. Letuij—Juliet.
4. Natyonh—Anthony.
5. Obza—Boaz.
6. Emoro—Romeo.
7. Artapocle—Cleopatra.
8. Cap ill, sir?—Priscilla.
9. Jo, Ned, n Hal—John Alden.
10. Cobaj—Jacob.
11. Helcar—Rachel.
12. Chunp—Punch.
13. Duyj—Judy.
14. Lonepano—Napoleon
15. Nosehijep—Josephine.

TO MATCH PARTNERS

Have two baskets containing tiny red hearts on which are written the names of famous lovers of history or fiction. The boys draw from one basket, the girls from another. Then Romeo seeks Juliet; Hamlet, Ophelia; John Alden, Priscilla; Dante, Beatrice; Leicester, Queen Elizabeth; Petrarch, Laura; Ivanhoe, Rowena; Hiawatha, Minnehaha; Othello, Desdemona; Robert Browning, Elizabeth Barrett; Jack, Jill; Gabriel, Evangeline; Paul, Virginia; Jacob, Rachel; the Prince, Cinderella; David Copperfield, Dora; and Punch, Judy.

THE LIVING VALENTINE

A game of interest used by one League was "The Living Valentine." There was an empty picture frame, behind which each one stood, in turn, while the others tried to make the "living valentine" laugh. All sorts of things happened, many funny things were said, and no one stood the test very long. The winner of the prize offered stood a little over a minute without laughing.—*Gladys Wheeler, Berlin, Ga.*

WASHINGTON'S BIRTHDAY SOCIAL

Write the invitations on small cardboard hatchets. You might request the guests to wear colonial costumes.

Use plenty of bunting, flags, etc., for decorations. Have a large picture of Washington draped with bunting. George and Martha might receive the guests.

Collection of Revolutionary Relics.—Have catalogues typewritten, setting forth this great collection of colonial antiquities. Appoint some person as guide and have the company visit the exhibit in groups.

1. The Early Home of George Washington.
2. Washington Crossing the Delaware.
3. The Old Colonel.
4. True Blue.
5. Vision of Washington's Old Age.
6. The Most Brilliant Light of Washington's Era.
7. The Lone Picket.
8. Down on the Suwannee River.
9. The Tax on Tea.
10. The Old Times and the New.

To represent these you would have: 1. An old-fashioned cradle. 2. The word "Washington" written on a slip of paper and placed across the map of Delaware. 3. A dried-up corn kernel. 4. A bottle of bluing. 5. A pair of spectacles. 6. A candle. 7. A fence picket. 8. A downy feather on a map of Georgia on which the Suwannee River is evident. 9. Some tacks on the letter T or on a saucer containing a bit of tea. 10. An old and new copy of a paper named the *Times.*

You may add to this list or substitute others for the

ones given at your pleasure. A little thought will suggest some exhibits you can use.

Living Pictures.—Nothing is more entertaining than cleverly presented living pictures. Get some one to make a huge frame. Stand this out from the wall some distance, say ten feet, with long sticks running back on either side from the top of the frame to the wall, helping to hold the frame in place. These sticks also serve as a framework for the top and side covering. Drop dark-colored blankets down from the sticks to cover the sides, and cover the top by spreading blankets across. Of course any dark-colored heavy cloth will do for this covering of sides and top. Cover the front of the frame with mosquito netting. Drape a large box at the back of this inclosure to serve as a platform on which the participants may pose. Arrange for a light to shine inside the inclosure and upon the poser. Have the frame curtained off, letting pages in colonial costume pull the curtain aside when the picture is ready to show. All lights should be turned off while the picture is being presented except the light that is to shine on the picture. If the instructions are followed as outlined, the tableaux will be very effective.

Put on the following program of songs and pictures:

1. A Revolutionary Belle.
2. An Old-Time Beau.
3. Solo or quartet, "Love's Old Sweet Song."
4. A Continental Soldier.
5. The Cherry Tree Scene.
6. The Soldier's Dream. (Have some one sing "Little Mother of Mine" while another poses as a sweet old lady sitting in a rocking-chair looking at a photograph of her boy.)
7. Tenting To-night. (Show three or four boys, either in colonial uniform or in khaki, sitting around a camp fire, which may be produced by the use of some sticks, a

bit of red tissue or crêpe paper, an extension cord, and an electric light globe. Have a male quartet sing "Tenting To-Night.")

8. Columbia. (Tack a large American flag across the back to serve as a background for this picture, which should come as the climax of your entertainment. Have every one stand and sing "The Star-Spangled Banner.")

Refreshments, cherry ice and cake.

ADDITIONAL WASHINGTON'S BIRTHDAY SUGGESTIONS

Washington

Let each one see how many words he can make out of the word "Washington."

Flag Relay

Have several teams of from five to ten runners each. The teams line up with the first runner on each team toeing the mark. Opposite each line is a tiny flag stuck in a half potato and standing erect on the floor. The first runner on each team at the signal runs to his flag, picks it up, and carries it back to the next runner, who in the meantime has moved up to the starting line. No. 2 starts as soon as he has been handed the flag, carries it back to the potato, sticks it in its original place, and rushes back to touch off No. 3, who in turn has moved up to the starting point. No. 3 gets the flag, hands it to No. 4, and so on. The first team to cover the course in this manner wins.

Patriotic Anagrams

Lettered chips of cardboard are faced down on a table. Some one turns up a chip, showing the letter. The first player to call some word of patriotic suggestion receives the chip. The winner is the player with the greatest number of chips at the close of the game.

This game may be played progressively, piles of chips being placed on several tables. The players would count chips after a few minutes of play, note the number on a tally card, put back all chips, and allow the girl and boy with the highest score to progress to the next table. After twenty or thirty minutes of actual play, the game is called, scores totaled, and the winner announced.

Playing the War Game

Provide each player with pencil and paper. Hang the following questions pertaining to the war on the wall (allow a specified time for answering):

1. A part of the body and a vowel.
2. Light knocks.
3. An English river and parts of the human body.
4. A boy's head covering and two thousand pounds.
5. A month.
6. To hinder and to help.
7. The inside of a nut.
8. A popular "movie" star.
9. A short sleep and what flour comes in.
10. A carousal and a great Southern soldier.

1. Army (arm-e). 2. Taps. 3. Defeat (Dee-feet). 4. Captain (cap-ton). 5. March. 6. Blockade. 7. Colonel (kernel). 8. Chaplain (Chaplin). 9. Knapsack (napsack). 10. Reveille (Revel-Lee).

KEWPIE SOCIAL FOR FEBRUARY

Kewpie is Cupid brought up to date, so why not have a Kewpie social for Valentine night? Kewpie is Cupid in caricature, a sort of funny-page edition, and he has grown mighty popular in the last few years. He would serve well as the central figure around which to plan your February social.

Invitation.—Posters might be used in conspicuous places. A cut-out picture of Kewpie pasted on cardboard would make the setting for one of these posters. The following wording would complete your poster:

> "Brother, Sister, we've been thinking
> What a shame if you'd forget
> To come to our Kewpie social;
> It's the best that we've had yet."

Kutie Kewpies.—All have been requested to bring baby photographs of themselves. These are turned in to the committee on arrival. The committee numbers and registers them as they are received, placing the proper name beside each number on a list kept for the purpose of checking up on the answers made by the guests. After most of the guests have arrived, place the pictures on exhibit, supply the crowd with paper and pencils, and have them guess who the different "Kuties" are. After a specified time, read the correct list in the hands of the committee and let each person check up on his own list. The person having the list most nearly correct should be recognized as the "Champeen Kutie" and should be appropriately decorated with such insignia as will attest that fact. A crown, badge, or medal with suitable inscription would answer the purpose.

If the photographs could be got together before the evening of the social and properly numbered and listed, so much the better.

Kewpie Set-Up Race.—Divide the crowd into two camps, the Kewpies and the Billikins. Ten representatives from each camp now engage in a race, lining up behind the starting line. Across the room, opposite each line of contestants, has been drawn a circle about eighteen inches in diameter. Outside each circle stand three Indian clubs dressed in ballet skirts of tissue paper to represent Kewpies.

The race is conducted in relay fashion. The first man on each team runs to his circle, places the "Kewpies" in upright position within the circle, and then rushes back to touch off the next runner in line. This player must be standing with both feet back of the starting line and is not privileged to run until his team-mate touches his outstretched hand. He proceeds to set up the "Kewpies" outside the circle once more. Thus it goes until all the members of the team have run. All "Kewpies" must be in upright position before a player can proceed farther. Should one fall after being set up, the runner must return and place it again in upright position before being allowed to touch off the next runner.

The members of the winning team should be decorated with long cheesecloth sashes tied in big rows at the back. These should be worn the rest of the evening.

Kewpie Quoits.—Six heart-shaped quoits should be made of heavy wire. Three of these should be covered with blue ribbon and three with pink. A gilt arrow should be made of wood and fastened to a base. This will then serve as a peg at which to toss the quoits. The Kewpies and Billikins again contest, every player being allowed a chance to toss the three quoits belonging to his side. Each ringer counts one point for the side. A box of heart-shaped mints may be given to the winning side.

Kewpie Cut-Outs.—Form two concentric circles with boys on the outside and girls on the inside. Let them march to music in opposite directions. When the music stops, the marchers stop and face one another. The couples thus formed are supplied with a piece of stiff paper eight by six inches and a piece of tissue paper somewhat larger. Each girl has been requested to bring a pair of scissors with ner to the social. Out of this material the girl is to cut a Kewpie and the boy is to dress it. Judges decide which is the best. Ten-cent store Kewpie dolls may be awarded the winners.

Kewpie Telegrams.—The same couples are furnished paper and pencils and told to write telegrams, using as initials the six letters K-E-W-P-I-E, thus: "Keep everything. Wrong Prices in Envelope." Have each telegram read aloud. The vote of the crowd may be taken as to the best.

Kewpie Fortunes.—Kewpie dolls or paper imitations should be arranged in marked-off spaces on a table. Each should be dressed in a different color. One at a time the guests are blindfolded, turned about, and told to place one hand on the table. The Kewpie occupying the space indicates the fortune in a message printed in large letters on a card hanging from his neck. It may be advisable to change the position of the Kewpies every now and then to keep the players guessing. The Kewpies tell the fortunes in the following words:

"Kewpie red,
Soon will wed.

Kewpie blue,
Lover true.

Kewpie green,
She's a queen.

(He'll be mean.)

Kewpie white,
Life-long fight.

Kewpie black,
Never lack.

Kewpie pink,
Twice, I think."

Kewpie Jingle.—Each person is given a slip of paper on which are typewritten the verses of the Kewpie jingle, the last word in each line being omitted. These are to be filled in by the guests with double letters of the alphabet as indicated in the parenthesis. The person with the nearest correct list may be given some little book of jingles.

There was a Kewpie who was —— (YY)
  Enough to take no —— (EE)
And study lovers with his —— (II)
  And think on what he —— (CC).

He saw a lot of foolish —— (JJ)
  Who always liked to —— (TT).
It really seemed to be the cr—(AA),
  A case of heart dis—(ZZ).

Then Kewpie did his wise head —— (UU),
  Got busy as the —— (BB);
So really there was no ex—(QQ)
  To dodge the marriage f—(EE).

Now one married jay, who ar—(OO)
  Spoke angrily this —— (YY):
I here and now prop—(OO)
  To black this Kewpie's —— (II).

(Apologies to Bancroft.)

Refreshments.—Kewpie tonic (sweet milk) and life-savers (doughnuts), the latter especially for those who are getting out in deep water, may be served as refreshments.

VALENTINE PARTY

Invitation

"Sir Valentine is Cupid's mate,
  And they work right together;
Each boy and girl, come out posthaste,
  Whatever be the weather;

Valentine Day we'll celebrate
With games and hearty laughter;
Next Tuesday night we'll meet at eight;
Don't come a minute after."

Valentine Quartets

Cut a number of comic valentines in four parts each. Hide the parts about the room. Begin your social by having all guests hunt for them. When a player has obtained one of the valentine parts, he proceeds to hunt for the persons with the other three parts. The first quartet to put together its valentine may be given some award. Note that it will be necessary to estimate your crowd before hiding the valentine parts that they may come out evenly.

When the quartets have formed, announce that each group is to write a valentine couplet—that is, a rhyme of two lines. You might write a few words on the board as suggestions. Heart, dart; love, dove; mine, pine; thine, valentine—perhaps these would do. The quartet with the best couplet should be presented with a small box of candy hearts.

Pitching Hearts

Divide the crowd into two groups by having them line up and count off. All the even numbers will form one group and all the odds another. Furnish one side with tiny cardboard hearts of white or pink, and the other side with hearts of red, three to each player. Standing at a distance of some five or six feet, the players, one at a time, try to toss these hearts into a small basket or into one of those large heart-shaped candy boxes. After all players have participated, the hearts are counted to determine which side is winner.

Valentine Puzzle

Paste five or more comic valentines on a cardboard. Cut them in small pieces in picture-puzzle fashion. There should be five or more tables, with not more than five players to a table, and a puzzle for each table. In case of necessity, the number of players at a table may be increased. Each player at the table takes his turn putting the puzzle together. Some one in the group acts as time-keeper, marking down the time required by each one. The player at the table with the fastest time is winner. The winners from the various tables then engage in an elimination contest to determine the champion at the game.

Sir Valentine

This is an adaptation of the old game, "Who, Sir? I, Sir?" The players stand or sit in a line and count off, each remembering his number. One player stands in front of the line and says: "Sir Valentine has lost his love, all on account of No. 1." Immediately his number is called, No. 1 must say: "Who, sir? I, sir?" "Yes, sir! You, sir!" says Sir Valentine. "No, sir! Not I, sir!" "Who, then, sir?" "No. 6, sir."

Immediately his number is mentioned, No. 6 must say, "Who, sir? I, sir?" and the above dialogue is repeated, and so on, until some player is caught off his guard and Sir Valentine is enabled to command said player to go foot before he can respond.

If No. 6, for instance, should be napping when his number is called by No. 1, Sir Valentine would command, "No. 6, go foot!" before he could get out his "Who, sir? I, sir?" No. 6 then takes his place at the foot, and all the players that had been below him move up one, and thus their numbers are changed. If Sir Valentine works rapidly, the game will move along merrily.

In very large crowds several groups should be formed with a Sir Valentine for each group.

This is a rousing good game and keeps the players constantly on the alert lest they be sent to the foot. Should a player fail to use "sir" in the proper place, he is also demoted.

Valentine Fortunes

Paste on a large heart valentines or pictures representing the following: An old maid, a moneybag, a bride, a laborer, a wedding bell, a wedding ring. Hang this heart on the wall. The players are blindfolded, one at a time, and sent toward the heart to touch one of the pictures with the index finger. This tells the fortune in the following manner:

Old Maid.
"Since the old maid you choose,
All chances you will lose."

Moneybag.
"Riches will come to you some day,
By marriage or another way."

Bride.
"Happy marriage will be your lot;
Fortune will frown on your rival's plot."

Laborer.
"Hard work is writ in destiny
For you, in winning victory."

Wedding Bell.
"For you this year the chimes will ring;
They're wedding bells and everything."

Wedding Ring.
"Don't be discouraged; don't you fret;
For some poor soul you may fool yet."

These fortunes may be written in large letters beneath the pictures they represent.

A Violet Romance

This clever contest was used at one party we attended. The story was typewritten on small, white sheets of paper. These sheets were attached to a purple paper cover and was then folded. In the upper left-hand corner of the white sheet were two cleverly made paper violets, tied with a bit of yellow baby ribbon. Blank spaces in the romance were left to be filled in with words formed from the letters in the word "violet." (The italics indicate the words to be omitted.)

"O *let* me now narrate to you
The story of a *love* so true.
A youth named *Leo* once did dwell;
His daily *toil* he did full well.
No *evil* ways had he forsooth;
He was indeed a model youth.
To win a maiden he did try,
With others eagerly did *vie;*
Alas! the light of hope grew dim;
The tender *tie* was not for him.
He lost his maid he loved so well,
And this is how that *it* befell:
Quoth she: 'Look you with favoring mind
Upon the vote for womankind?'
'No,' he replied, 'I'll tell you flat,
I never fail to *veto* that.'
So ended then the romance brief;
Instead of joy he found but grief."

CHAPTER III

MARCH PROGRAMS

IRISH BUBBLE PARTY

Why not have something different for your St. Patrick's social? Young folks get tired of the stereotyped "programmy" affairs we so often palm off on them for socials. How about an "Irish Bubble Party"?

The Social Committee should meet and make enough tissue paper hats to provide one for everybody who comes to the social. Half the hats should be green and half white. They should be numbered, the green set being numbered in doubles from one on up and likewise the white set. Thus there will be two greens numbered one, two numbered two, etc. There would also be two whites numbered one, two numbered two, etc. Every one who comes to the social is expected to wear one of these hats during the whole of the evening's fun. The hats should be kept in four separate piles, a boy's pile and a girl's pile for each color. The girl and boy having the same number and color become partners for the evening.

The social opens with a grand march around the room to a piano accompaniment, everybody singing "The Wearing of the Green" or some other appropriate song.

Then they are to gather at the several tables, on each of which are a bowl of soapsuds and a clay pipe for each player. The soap bubble contests then begin. Judges have been previously appointed.

1. *Largest Bubble.*—The person blowing the largest bubble at each table has a green ribbon bow tied on his pipe. These persons then contest, and the winner gets an additional bow.

2. *Partner Bubbles.*—Partners by putting their pipes close together may make one large bubble. The partners at each table making the largest bubble in this way get a green bow each. The winners then contest as before, and an extra green bow is allowed the winners of the final.

3. *Highest Bubble.*—The person at each table to blow the highest bubble gets a green bow in this contest. As in the other contests, the winners contest for the additional bow.

4. *Most Bubbles.*—The person who can blow the most bubbles from one dip into the solution wins in this event. Winners at the various tables again contest to decide the champion.

5. *Through Wreath.*—A wreath is hung in a convenient place, and each person able to blow a bubble through it gets a green bow.

6. *Bubble Tournament.*—The Greens and the Whites line up against each other in this contest, about one and one-half feet on each side of a rope or line stretched across the room. The Greens are furnished with fans, the Whites with pipes and bubble solution. For five minutes the

Whites blow bubbles and endeavor to have them break on the enemy's side of the line. The Greens with their fans endeavor to prevent this. Judges award one point for every bubble that breaks in Green territory. The situation is then reversed, and for five minutes more the Greens try to blow bubbles into the White camp.

The following is a good bubble solution recipe: Fill a preserve jar two-thirds full of boiling water. Add three ounces of castile soap finely shaven, a teaspoonful of sugar, and four tablespoonfuls of glycerin. Shake thoroughly and strain through a white cloth.

Care should be taken to cover all tables used with oilcloth or heavy paper.

Clay pipes may be gotten through some dealer in town at something like eighty-five cents per hundred at wholesale price.

Shamrocks or little white clay pipes with a tiny green ribbon bow may be given as souvenirs.

Refreshments: Sandwiches tied with green ribbon, olives, pickles, Irish potato chips, green tea, and green mints or candy. Brick ice cream would also be appropriate.

(This social may be used at any other time by eliminating the St. Patrick idea.)

Bubble Race

Let two contestants each represent four sides, say the Murphys, the Caseys, the O'Briens, and the O'Malleys. One contestant on each team has a fan; the other is the bubble blower. At a given signal contestants blow one bubble each, shake it off the pipe, and the fanner tries to waft it toward the designated goal line. The first over the line wins. If the bubble breaks, the fanner may come back to the starting point and get another bubble to start on its way.

Bubble Croquet

This contest may be held on a table covered with a woolen cloth, upon which ribbon-bound wickets are placed at intervals. Sides contest, and each player may blow three bubbles at a turn, endeavoring to fan or blow them through the wickets. Five points are counted if the bubble goes through one wicket, ten if it goes through two of them, and fifteen if it goes through the third one before bursting.

A PAT PARTY

"A great man was St. Pat,
We assure you of that,
And so we're givin' him a party,
To honor his name
And add to his fame,
And we're invitin' you, my hearty."

Have Pat and Biddy meet all the guests as they arrive, giving to each a shamrock or a tiny Irish flag or a bit of green ribbon to wear. Pat meets all the ladies, and Biddy attends to the "gintlemen."

Snake Hunt.—Cut out tapering pieces of green paper and hide them about the room. The guest that finds the most snakes may be given some sort of prize—a toy snake, for instance.

An Irish Potato Race.—Match the girls against the men in the following manner: Four chairs, two at each side of the room, are needed. On the chairs beside the contestants are three potatoes each. With a spoon these must be carried across to the opposite chair, deposited there, and then they must be brought back in like manner. Count the wins to decide whether the *Biddies* or the *Pats* are victors.

This contest may be run in relay style, one runner carrying them across the course and another bringing them back.

A "Pat" Contest.—Give out paper and pencil and put the following questions on the blackboard for answer:

1. Pat fighting for his country?
2. Pat grown haughty and of noble birth?
3. Pat playing with the baby?
4. Pat mending his clothing?
5. Pat with an ornamental quilt?
6. Pat protecting his own ingenuity?
7. Pat as the head of a family?
8. Pat in relation to his children?
9. Pat abroad speaking an inferior dialect?
10. Pat grown very old and with hoary locks.
11. Pat in uniform and on the force?
12. Pat at the dressmaker's?
13. Pat imitating raindrops?
14. Pat on the table?
15. Pat an object of sympathy?

1. Patriotic. 2. Patrician. 3. Pat-a-cake. 4. Patching. 5. Patchwork. 6. Patent. 7. *Paterfamilias.* 8. Paternal. 9. Patois. 10. Patriarch. 11. Patrol. 12. Pattern. 13. Patter. 14. Patty. 15. Pathetic.

Pat's Hat.—Have some one draw a funny Irishman wearing a plug hat on a square of white muslin. Each player in turn is given a shamrock and, blindfolded, attempts to pin it to Pat's hat. Those who succeed may draw for a prize.

Irish Tenpins.—Divide your crowd into two sides now —the Murphys and the Caseys—and let them engage in an Irish tenpin contest. The tenpins are numbered from 1 to 10, and contestants roll a long potato at them. A scorer will keep count and total the scores for each side.

Where tenpins or Indian clubs are not available, substitution may be made by putting up sticks on round bases.

Serve mint jello and "Killarney" cakes.

AN IRISH FROLIC

Invitation written in green ink: "Can yez attind a frolic and gineral divarsion on the 17th of March in the avenin'? Shure, 'tis wilcum ye'll be."

Have a supply of gold harps, green shamrocks, white pipes, and green snakes cut out of paper. Each person as he arrives has either a harp, a shamrock, a pipe, or a snake pinned on him. This service may be performed by two uniformed "cops" or by two Irish colleens wearing little green crêpe paper bonnets.

The groups now form, the crowd having been equally divided between the harps, the shamrocks, the pipes, and the snakes. As the Irish are strong on politics, each group may "ilict" a leader, at least two candidates running for leader of each group.

Irish Flag March.—Tiny Irish flags or square bits of green paper pasted on toothpicks have been stuck up about the room wherever possible. Some one plays the piano, and all four groups march around in a circle, clapping hands. When the music stops, which it does at unexpected intervals, all players scramble for the flags. Immediately the music strikes up all players must resume their marching and clapping. This continues until all the flags have been collected. The person with the largest number of flags is declared champion of Ireland. All flags in each group are also counted to determine which group is winner.

A Green Contest.—Each group is furnished the following list of questions, which must be answered in a specified time, the entire group working together on it (all answers contain the word "green" or its equivalent):

1. Suggestive of an apple? Greening.
2. Suggestive of a well-known poet? John Greenleaf Whittier.
3. One of our national defenses? Fort Greene.
4. A valuable paper? Greenback.
5. A town in Kentucky, Texas, and many other States? Greenville.
6. Suggestive of flowers? Greenhouse.
7. Easily hoodwinked? Greenhorn.
8 Part of the rainbow? Green.
9. Suggestive of a plum? Greengage.
10. A country? Greenland.
11. Suggestive of a theater? Greenroom.
12. A green that's jealous? Green-eyed.
13. A green that beautifies a country home? Greensward.
14. A green used extensively in the war? Grenade.

The answers are read, each group marking its own paper and announcing how many answers were correct.

The Blarney Race.—Each group is represented in the blarney race by a girl and a boy. The girls are lined up at one side of the room, the boys at the other. At a given signal each girl starts for her partner, holding in her hand a sealed envelope containing a single easy word. He must open the envelope and write a complimentary couplet as quickly as possible, using the word he finds in the envelope for the rhyme. For instance, the word in the envelope may be "pink." So he may write:

"O lassie divine, with cheeks so pink,
You're the sweetest girl in town, I think."

The girl then rushes back to the starting point with this bit of blarney, the first one back being declared winner. All couplets are then read to the crowd.

Irish Golf.—Allow the sides now to contest in a game of Irish golf. Of course a small potato is used as a golf ball. A lath with a piece tacked to it at one end at right angles will serve as a golf stick. The golf course is represented by five tomato cans, one in the center and the four at equal distances out from it on four sides. These cans should have a section cut out of the side so that when the can is stood upright the "golf" ball may be driven into it. Contestants will start at the center and make a round in this manner: Ball is shoved or driven out from No. 1

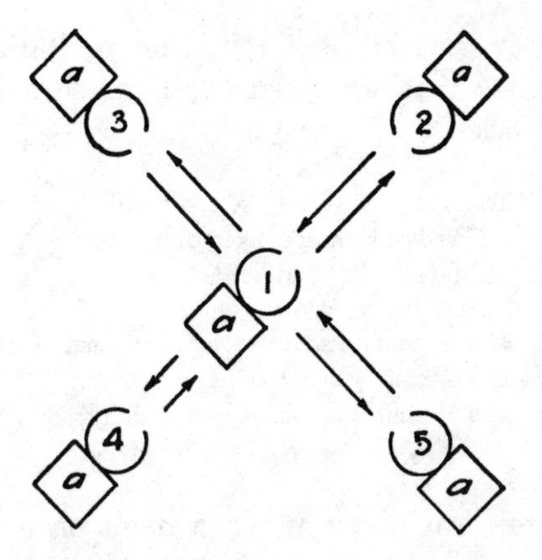

to No. 2. When the player has gotten the ball into No. 2, he drives it back to No. 1, then to No. 3 and back to center, to No. 4 and center, to No. 5 and center. Each time the player must "hole" the ball before proceeding. The number of strokes required to complete the course marks the player's score. The group that finishes with the lowest score is declared the winner. The champion Irish golf player may also be determined by the individual scores. Players play one at a time. If desired, a certain number of players may represent each group. It might be well to tack each can to a block of wood at the back (*a*) to keep it from toppling over. The can in the center will then have to be turned at the pleasure of the "golfer."

Announce which group scored the most points during the evening. Serve some sort of lettuce sandwiches and "tay," finishing up with green mints.

MISCELLANEOUS

An Invitation

One Society sent out the following invitation to a St. Patrick's party. It was written in green ink on white paper shamrocks:

"The 16th of March in the avenin'
Has been chosen by a few
To have a St. Patrick's party,
And we're invitin' you.
Please come and wear an Irish smile;
We want you on the scene.
You'll find the place quite aisily;
'Twill all be trimmed in green."

Each person was given an Irish name on entering, and the boys were told to go to an arranged post office, where they were to secure the names of their partners and green hats for them to wear. Irish games were played, the concluding feature being the bubble tournament as outlined in the Irish Bubble Party.

An Irish Gathering

Divide the party into groups—the Maloneys, Murphys. Kellys, etc. Each family group will be composed of father, mother, and five or six children or relatives, the number in the family depending on the size of the crowd.

Each family group is required to perform some stunt for the entertainment of the crowd.

Suggestive Words to Keep in Mind When Arranging for a St. Patrick's Social

Harp, shamrock, pig, pipe, Paddy hat, Biddy bonnet, frog, potato, snake, and shillalah.

Shamrock Aprons

Use large paper napkins or white tissue paper for skirt. Cut out enough green tissue paper shamrocks to make a border around the apron, which may be cut to shape desired. A double-fold strip of white tissue paper will serve as top of apron and belt. The shamrocks may be cut out of the decorated border in crêpe paper, if that is available. It would be lots of fun to let the boys make these aprons for the girls to wear.

Irish Melodies

Some one at the piano plays a few bars from each of a dozen Irish melodies. Players guess what they are and write down the names.

Snakes St. Patrick Drove Out of Ireland

1. Worn a few years back in winter time by women? Boa.
2. Worn all the year round? Garter.
3. Baby plays with it and never gets hurt? Rattle.
4. Expensive to feed in these days of high cost of living? Egg eater.
5. How Fritz would describe a napkin? Viper.
6. A short-winded mathematician? Puffing adder.
7. An Indian wears it with comfort? Moccasin.

8. A nickname given to Northern sympathizers with the South during the Civil War? Copperhead.

9. A very fast horse? Racer.

Matching Green

Six samples of different shades of green cloth and two squares of pasteboard. Cut samples in half. Paste one-half on one piece of cardboard and one-half on the other. Mark one set with letters or Roman numerals and the other with numbers, taking care that the matching pieces do not correspond except that they may correspond in one shade as a "catch." One piece of cardboard is hung on one side of the room and the other across from it. Paper and pencils are given the players, and they are asked to write down the matching halves—thus, A-2, B-1, etc. Players whose answers are correct may draw for a prize of some sort.

Irish Potato Race

"Praties" may be propelled over the course with wands decorated with bows of green ribbon. Or the ordinary potato race may be run, setting out a row of five potatoes for each contestant. These are to be brought back one at a time and deposited in a basket, the first player finishing by getting all his potatoes in the basket in this manner winning. This may be varied by requiring contestants to hop or to carry the potatoes in a spoon.

Potato

Give five minutes for players to make as many words as possible out of the letters in the word "potato."

Animal Show

Let players gather around a table on which are placed peanuts, raisins, prunes, a bunch of wooden toothpicks, wire hairpins, etc. Each player receives a potato, out of which he must fashion an animal or hobgoblin of some sort, using the peanuts and fruit for heads and the toothpicks for limbs, tails, etc., as fancy dictates. At the end of ten minutes the different animals are arranged on the table for exhibition, and judges award prizes to those that seem the funniest. It may be possible afterwards to donate all the potatoes to some poor family, first giving the potatoes a washing.

Kissing the Blarney Stone

Whoever kisses the blarney stone will ever after say nothing but pleasant words.

Get a smooth white stone. Scrub it well. Place it in the center of a small table. Blindfold the players and let them attempt to kiss it, no feeling about for location being allowed. The fairies say those who kiss the blarney stone will be successful ever afterwards.

The spirit of contest may be injected into it by dividing into sides and awarding points for each successful attempt.

Pig

1. To draw a pig while blindfolded.
2. To pin tail on a pig while blindfolded.

Harp

Each player in turn is given a piece of chalk, blindfolded, and told to draw a straight line to represent a string in an outlined harp on the board.

What Irish Towns Mean

1. A sovereign and a city? Queenstown.
2. A stopper? Cork.
3. The capital of Ireland? Dublin.

4. A popular girl and speedy? Belfast.
5. A garment that protects from rough weather? Ulster.
6. To be cunning and to depart? Sligo.
7. To slay and to venture? Kildare.

Irish Songs

A pleasing program of Irish songs could be arranged. There's something about the lilt and melody of an Irish song that always charms. Such songs as "Kathleen Mavourneen," "The Harp That Once Through Tara's Halls," "The Wearing of the Green," and "My Wild Irish Rose" might be used, as well as some of the popular Irish ballads of recent years. "Mother Machree" would be in this class. Get some songs on your program that every one can sing.

Refreshment Suggestions

Pistachio ice cream, cakes with green icing, mint jello, lettuce sandwiches with mayonnaise dressing, green mints, green stick candy, olives, pickles, blarney sandwiches (tongue and chopped olives), and Hibernian or Irish punch. The latter is made in the following way: Make a strong lemonade, add a pint of lime juice, the juice of six oranges, and two grapefruit. Add plenty of crushed ice and water to suit taste.

A PIG PARTY

Invitation

"It's going to be a Pig Party,
And it's going to be a big party;
So you'd better get your rig, my hearty,
And come along."

Admission, One Grunt.

Costumes

All girls should be asked to come wearing gingham dresses with their hair plaited in pigtails. All boys should be asked to wear green ties and green vests if possible. It would be easy to cover the vests with green cheesecloth or crêpe paper.

Games

Pig in the Parlor

This makes a good game to start off the evening's fun, since it will serve as a good mixer. The crowd forms a circle with one player in the center. They take hold of hands and skip around the player in the center as they sing to the tune commonly used for "We Won't Get Home Until Morning":

"Got a pig in the parlor,
Got a pig in the parlor,
Got a pig in the parlor,
And he is Irish, too.

And he is Irish, too,
And he is Irish, too;
Got a pig in the parlor,
Got a pig in the parlor,
Got a pig in the parlor,
And he is Irish, too."

With the beginning of the next verse the players begin doing the grand right and left. Before starting, each player in the circle should have a partner, the boy being always at the girl's left. The grand right and left is done by all girls marching clockwise and all boys marching in the opposite direction, beginning by giving the partner the right hand and passing on, reaching the left hand to the next person coming toward you. Thus the players weave in and out, extending first the right hand and then the left. The player in the center drops into the line and participates in the march as they sing:

> "Right hand to your partner,
> Left hand to your neighbo ,
> Right hand to the next one,
> And all promenade."

At this last bit of advice to promenade each player seeks to get a partner and clasps hands with that person in skating position, marching or skipping then as they sing:

> "And all promenade,
> And all promenade;
> Got a pig in the parlor,
> Got a pig in the parlor,
> Got a pig in the parlor;
> We'll all promenade."

One player is left without a partner and goes to the center. The game is thus played over and over as long as desired.

If there are more girls than boys, let some of the girls tie handkerchiefs around their right arms and represent boys during the game.

Pig Artists

Hand each player a sheet of paper and a pencil. Request that each one, with eyes closed, draw a pig without lifting the pencil from the paper except to make the eye. Have them sign their names and write some short message beneath the picture. Let players exchange papers for their own edification. With a small crowd it may be possible to have all the drawings made in one book expressly fixed for the occasion. This book may be given as a prize to the one who makes the cleverest drawing.

Pig Race

Divide the crowd into two sides and have a pig race between representatives of the two groups. At intervals of several feet in two rows across the room place oyster crackers on pieces of paper. The racers must hop to the crackers one after another, stoop without touching the raised foot to the floor, pick the cracker up with the mouth, and eat it. Or they may be required to race on all fours.

Pigtail Quartet

Four girls with fairly good voices and pigtails stand in a row with their backs to the crowd. The director pulls the pigtails and the girls respond with some song such as "Anne Laurie" or "Old Folks at Home." By pulling two or more of the pigtails at once he gets his effects of harmony. The first number should be made as good as possible. After that a humorous number can be introduced, the quartet singing "Sweet Ivory Soap" or some such song. At the end the director could pull off a false pigtail worn by one of the girls.

Greasy Pig Relay

Have from ten to twenty players from each side line up, facing one another. The head player on each team would start on signal and zigzag down his line, running around each player. He zigzags back in like manner to his original position. Immediately upon reaching his original position the player to his right does the same thing, zigzagging until he returns to his original position, not neglecting to run around the player at the head before finishing. The first team to have all its players perform in this manner wins the race.

Pinning on a Pigtail

This would be like the old game of pinning on the

donkey's tail. The pigtail could be made by wrapping a piece of wire around a piece of hemp rope and giving it the desired curl. Let your best artist draw with charcoal a large-sized pig on a piece of muslin.

Pig in the Pen

Players stand in groups of three. Two hold hands and form the pen. The third is the pig and stands inside the pen. One odd pig is without a pen. On signal, which may be given by a whistle, all pigs must change pens, the odd pig trying to get a pen in the scramble. The one left out becomes odd pig, and the game starts over. Players forming the pens should change with the pigs occasionally that all may get the chance to be pigs.

Another way to play this game is to introduce a chaser. The odd pig may save himself from being tagged by dodging into a pen. The pig in that pen must vacate immediately and flee from the chaser. Should a pig be tagged he becomes chaser immediately and the chaser becomes pig. The game is most fun when the changes from one pen to another are rapid.

Pig and Pie

Have two or three boys representing each side engage in a pie-eating contest. The pies should be covered with meringue, and the contestants should be required to eat with their hands tied behind them.

Pigtail Race

Have from six to ten players represent each side. They divide up equally, and half the players line up at one end of the room and half at the other. The pigtails are made of heavy cardboard and are about one yard in length. Be careful to see that all of them are the same length. The first player on each team is given two such pigtails. At the signal he starts across the room, laying the two pigtails end to end across the room. It is not allowable to lift one of the pigtails until the other is lying flat on the floor. Reaching the opposite side of the room, the player hands both pigtails to his team-mate there as soon as he touches the goal line. This player then starts back to the other side, measuring off in the same manner. And thus it goes until all players have covered the distance.

Feeding the Pigs

Have several couples represent each side. Blindfold them and furnish each person with a spoon and a bowl filled with cracker crumbs mixed with molasses. On signal all contestants start feeding their partners.

A Pig Contest

1. A pig that's a bird. (Pigeon.)
2. A pig that's useful to artists. (Figment.)
3. A pig that is dwarfish. (Pigmy.)
4. A pig that interests healthy boys. (Pigskin.)
5. A Chinese pig. (Pigtail.)

Refreshments

Serve pig sandwiches (barbecued pork) and coffee.

CHAPTER IV

APRIL PROGRAMS

A TANGLE PARTY

How about a tangle party for this month?

Invitation:

"NEGLAT TARPY"

"Get all the kinks out of your disposition, untangle your feet, and come to our tangle party. Don't get all tangled up about the date. It's to happen Friday evening, May 14.

"Sunday school room, eight o'clock."

TANGLED SONGS

Copy and cut into four pieces the lines to the chorus of some familiar song. Distribute the pieces promiscuously and have the crowd match them, thus forming numerous groups of four each. Each group now must render its song. Insist on each member of the group taking part. After the groups have rendered the songs separately, have them all sing together, each group singing its own song as lustily as is possible.

Cobweb Tangle

Use the old cobweb social idea, winding strings all over one side of the room, over chairs, under tables, over pictures, up- and downstairs, through doors, criss-crossing, tangling with other strings, etc. Each person takes hold of an end of the string and follows it to the other end, winding it around the hands as they proceed. Have a stick of candy or a sack of peanuts or a peanut shell with a fortune in it tied at the end of each string.

Tangled Stunt

Play "Hurly Burly." All the players stand in a circle. Each is given something to do by the leader, who whispers to each one. When all have been instructed the leader shouts "Hurly Burly," and each one performs the stunt assigned him.

Some have been asked to run in a circle, some to crawl, some to bray, some to crow, some to jump an imaginary rope, some to prance up and down, etc. You can imagine what a sight it would be to have them all doing these different stunts at one time.

Tangled Characters

1. Rodowow Isnowl.
2. Redoohet Tovosleer.
3. Dloly Oregeg.
4. Terrebh Voreoh.
5. Loneopan.
6. Nollinc.
7. Hastingonw.
8. Hirsengp.
9. Hocf.
10. Malliwi Ginsnenj Naryb.

1. Woodrow Wilson. 2. Theodore Roosevelt. 3. Lloyd George. 4. Herbert Hoover. 5. Napoleon. 6. Lincoln. 7. Washington. 8. Pershing. 9. Foch. 10. William Jennings Bryan.

(Tangled cities may be worked out in the same way and substituted for tangled characters.)

Hand each person a list of the tangled characters and give some award for the first correct untangled list.

Tangled Answers

Have each boy write a question and each girl an answer on a slip of paper. Let some one collect all the questions, mix them in a hat, and have each boy draw one. In like manner let some one collect the answers and redistribute them to the girls. Now have each boy ask the question on his slip of the girl opposite him. She in turn reads the answer given her. Let this be done loud and clear enough for every one to hear.

Weaver's Relay

If you have plenty of room, divide your crowd into two circles and let them contest in the weaver's relay race. One person drops back out of each circle. At the signal to go each starts weaving in and out of his circle in under the clasped hands of the two back of whom he stands, and out under the next, and so on until he arrives back at his original position in the circle. As soon as he resumes his place in the circle the person to his right begins the weaving process and so on until all the players have run. The first side to have all the players run in this manner wins.

Tangled Partners

Now have half as many strings as there are persons present. These should be cut about two feet in length and run through a hole in the center of a bit of paper. Suspend this from a chandelier or in a doorway. Have the girls stand on one side and the boys on the other. Each girl and boy takes hold of an end of a string. When all have done so tell them to pull. The paper will be rent asunder, and the persons holding the same string are partners for the serving of refreshments.

Refreshments

The boys now retire from the room to reappear shortly, each with an apron on backward and each bearing a plate of refreshments for his partner. It would add to the fun if they backed in. After the girls are served the boys provide for themselves.

Grape juice and cake would make simple and inexpensive refreshments.

AN APRIL FISH PARTY

"Poisson D'Avril" (April Fish) the French say instead of "April Fool." The inference is that they are easily caught. A fish in that country is typical of the day. So why not cut out paper fish and write your invitations on them?

Following up the fish idea, hand to guests portions of cardboard or paper fish and tell them to match for partners. You may arrange it so boys will find boys for partners and girls will discover that they match up with other girls. Or you may arrrange it so no two parts match, and after there has been sufficient scramble for partners you may call "April Fool." In case the latter plan is used, add zest to the scramble by announcing a prize for the first two to match up as partners.

Still following up the "fish" idea, announce a "fishing trip." Have tiny paper fish hid in every conceivable place about the room. Every one joins in the "fishing trip" and of course endeavors to "catch" as many fish as possible. At the close of this game award a prize to the one who has the *smallest* number of fish.

Fix up a booth or corner of the room and display this sign in front of it: "Step in and See the Big Fish." A large mirror faces the victim as soon as he steps inside. Across it is written "April Fool."

Fishing.—Now allow the company to do some fishing by answering the following questions with the names of fish:

1. A prolonged cry? Wail (whale).
2. A choir singer? Bass.
3. The mariner's dread? Rock.
4. It's awful slippery? Eel.
5. It's a good idea sometimes to come down off it? Perch.
6. An animal that has practically disappeared? Buffalo.
7. A persistent serenader? Cat.
8. What we are liable to do in deep mud? Flounder.
9. A weapon of warfare that's more ornamental than useful in these times? Sword.
10. Mother's pride? Son (sun).
11. Sometimes they shoot? Star.
12. A censorious, complaining fish? Carp.
13. A household pet? Dog.
14. A swindler? Shark.

A fish Relay.—Divide the company into several groups —the whales, the sharks, the eels, the buffaloes, etc.—and let four girls and four boys represent each group in a fish relay. Each girl is provided with a glass of water and a teaspoon. At the signal the first girl on each team begins feeding her partner the water, a teaspoonful at a time.

As soon as this couple finishes it must sing to the tune of "We Won't Go Home Until Morning":

"One is born every minute,
One is born every minute,
One is born every minute,
And that ain't telling no lie."

Not until they have finished this can the next couple begin, and so on. The team finishing first marches around the other teams singing "One is born every minute."

Boys' Fishing Contest.—Now let all the girls gather in one room and all the boys in another. Two at a time the boys are to be invited into the room where the girls are, and there they engage in a fishing contest. Two chairs are provided, as well as two fishponds (inverted shoe or suit boxes with slits cut in them, out of which cardboard fish protrude a few inches). A hole is punched in the fish's head, and a fishing line and bent pinhook are provided each fisher. The rules of the contest require the fishing to be done with one eye shut. To make sure that the contestants don't peep, two girls are appointed to hold their right hands over each boy's right eye. The palms of these hands have been previously smutted. The victims are allowed to remain in the room while others are brought in. Of course they must not allow the newcomers to see what has befallen them.

Fishing for Partners.—Let the boys now fish for partners, a screen being put in front of the door of the room where the girls are and each boy in turn dropping a fishing line over the screen. Some girl takes hold of it and becomes his partner for refreshments.

Serve "sinkers" (doughnuts) and "angler's tea" (lemonade poured out of a jug) for refreshments.

AN APRIL FOOL PARTY

Have all sorts of April fool traps about the room.

1. A handkerchief tacked to the floor.

2. A mirror badly "cracked" by use of strips of paper and soap.

3. A box of good candy labeled "Take one" will last surprisingly long.

Give each guest a fool's cap of red and white crêpe paper. This is to be worn during the evening.

The hostess may present to guests as they arrive a hand which comes off, to the amazement of the new arrival. This may be arranged by stuffing a long glove and holding it on a stick so as to conceal the real hand.

Ask each one to write down the most foolish thing he or she ever did. Collect and read papers, asking players to guess the authorship of each one.

Have a doll-dressing contest for all the boys, furnishing each one with a peanut, some tissue or crêpe paper, needle, thread, pen and ink. Put them on exhibition and let the girls vote for the cleverest creation. Give as a prize a neatly wrapped box which, on being opened, is found to contain nothing.

Divide the crowd now into two groups, the Jesters and the Jokes, by having them draw slips from a hat. Each group may be asked to put on a stunt. They may also engage in the following contests:

Girls' Whistling Contest.—This may be conducted in one of two ways. (1) Select one or more girl contestants from each group. Let them stand facing the rest of the company and at a given signal begin whistling. It doesn't matter what they whistle. The girl that continues whistling for the longest time wins. Opposing "rooters" may do all manner of things to make whistlers laugh. (2) Have one girl and one boy represent each group. The girls toe the mark, the boys being across the room directly opposite their partners. Each girl is given a sealed envelope and at a given signal must run across to her partner, open the envelope, and whistle the tune indicated on a slip of paper inside the envelope. As soon as the boy recognizes the tune he writes the name of it on a slip of paper and hands it to the girl, who slips it into the envelope and races back to the starting point. The first to get back with the correct tune wins. Have some one present the winner with a fancy dish purchased at the ten-cent store. As he is about to hand it to her he stumbles and drops the dish, breaking it, seems disconcerted for a moment, but soon recovers himself and says, "April fool."

Fool Relay.—Select four contestants for each group. Have teams line up, with the first runners in line toeing the mark. Each player holds a cardboard letter, there being one "F," two "O's," and one "L," lining up in proper order, for each team. The contestants bearing "F" start walking to the designated goal in the following fashion: Four steps forward, about face, two steps back, about face, four steps forward, about face, two steps back, etc., until the goal is reached, when the contestant places his letter on the floor or sets it up against the wall, as the case may be, and returns, walking in the same manner. The second contestant has moved up to the starting line and starts as soon as No. 1 crosses the starting line. Each contestant must proceed as did No. 1, four steps forward, reverse, and two steps back. Mincing steps on the reverse movement are barred. The first team to spell "Fool" in this manner and have all its runners cover the course wins.

Obstacle Race.—Select one contestant from each group. Place a number of obstacles in the race course—buckets, books, cups, tumblers, etc. Let them try the course first, walking through it. Then blindfold contestants. Now have some one remove all obstacles noiselessly and start your race. If this is done cleverly enough, you will have some fancy high stepping to avoid knocking over or touching any of the obstacles, since one of the rules laid down is that each obstacle touched counts one point against the contestant. Contestants must walk and not attempt to run.

To get partners for refreshments have a number of strings three-quarters of a yard long. Shut them between folding doors or catch in any ordinary door, so that the ends hang on either side. The boys are on one side and the girls on the other. Each person takes hold of a string, and when doors are opened, or when the door is opened, persons found holding the same piece are partners.

Serve "tomato" salad, which proves to be a mixture of blood oranges, white grapes, and pecan nuts served in cucumber boats. Sandwiches with sliced bananas for filling will also be delightful. Sandwiches as slices of cake with nut filling wrapped in paper would also do.

Chocolate cigars and cigarettes may be given out.

April fool candy may be had at the candy store. It is well, however, in your serving to remember this bit of wisdom from some writer: "Let your guest be fooled by unexpected tastes, but not unpalatable ones."

APRIL FOOL SUGGESTIONS

Have misleading placards, directions on which lead the guests to unexpected places and mix the crowd.

Have crazy greetings about the room, such as "Happy New Year," etc.

Have a quartet which, after an elaborate prelude on the piano, during which they arrange themselves, open and close their mouths without a single sound and take their seats.

Have a *Backward Social.* Ask the girls to wear dresses

backward; the boys have their ties hanging down the back outside the coat. Let the players engage in a *Japanese Crab Race,* as described elsewhere in this book, or put on a *Japanese Crab Relay.*

Fix up ice cream to resemble croquettes by plentifully sprinkling the cone-shaped portions with toasted cake crumbs.

April Fool Statements

1. Jonah was an English poet.
2. Charlie Chaplin was once President of the United States.
3. John Bunyan is an ex-prize fighter champion.
4. John McCormick was a great inventor.
5. Theodore Roosevelt wrote "Pilgrim's Progress."
6. Thomas Edison was swallowed by a whale.
7. Billy Sunday wrote "Freckles."
8. James J. Corbett is a popular Irish tenor.
9. Alfred Tennyson is a popular movie actor.
10. Gene Stratton Porter was once a ball player.

Give paper and pencils to the players and have them correct these statements.

A RAINBOW PARTY

Invitations.—Use the following lines from Byron on your invitations:

> "Be thou my rainbow to the storms of life,
> The evening beam that smiles the clouds away
> And tints to-morrow with prophetic ray."

The rest of the invitation reads: "Rainbow Party, April 16 (name of organization, date and place).

Decorations.—Have a very riot of color everywhere. A huge rainbow can be effected by use of crêpe paper or cheesecloth in the seven prismatic colors. Over this draw a bit of white gauze to blend the colors.

The following are the prismatic colors that must be kept in mind in working out this social: Violet (purple), indigo (dark blue), blue (light), green, yellow, orange, red.

Rainbow Chase, or Seeking the Pot of Gold.—Hide somewhere in the room a thimble or something of the sort, representing the pot of gold at the foot of the rainbow. The players are to hunt for it. Each player as he finds it quietly takes his seat, not disturbing it and not tipping off other players as to its hiding place.

Bow Contest.—Give guests paper and pencil and a set of the following questions, which may be answered by words beginning or ending in "bow," "bo," or "beau":

1. An Old Testament bow? Boaz.
2. Appellation given by Christ to two fiery disciples? Boanerges.
3. A Hallowe'en bow? Bogy.
4. An unconventional bow? Bohemian.
5. A South American bow? Bolivia.
6. A sausage bow? Bologna.
7. A bow without fraud or deceit? *Bona fide.*
8. A rich yielding bow? Bonanza.
9. A military bow? Bonaparte.
10. A bow that's always acceptable? Bonus.
11. A poorly fed bow? Bony.
12. An acid bow? Boric.
13. An animal bow? Bovine.
14. A ne'er-do-well bow? Hobo.
15. A dandy bow? Beau Brummel.
16. A bow that is a dangerous weapon? Bowie knife.

Making Wishes.—The rainbow is a symbol of hope. Therefore a "wishing bee" would be appropriate. Let each person write a wish for some on else present, signing the name of that person. All papers are handed in and read to the crowd.

Rainbow Charades.—Number sets of slips from one to seven. Let players draw and then find the rest in their group. Thus there will be seven groups. After all the groups have gathered let the social chairman whisper to the leader of each group the name of one of the colors of the rainbow. Give each group a few moments now to plan for acting out the name of its color. The rest of the groups guess what color the group represents. A vote might be taken or judges may act to decide which group most cleverly represents its color. Some suggestions follow:

Purple (purr-pull).—Each of these syllables could be easily worked out.

Indigo (*Inn-dig-go*).—Have some wayworn travelers register at a country inn, etc.

Blue.—Group could sit about disconsolate and tell one another their troubles.

Green.—Have country boy show lack of knowledge of city ways or work "green" idea out in other ways.

Yellow (yell-o or low).—Have the group march about in a circle, giving some yell. Or after a yell let them proceed to pass under the clasped hands of two persons, the hands being held so low that they have to go under on all fours.

Orange (r-range).—Have the entire group do a bit of semaphore signaling by standing with arms extending straight out from the sides. This is R in the semaphore code. Then have boys pretend to be engaged in a battle with an unseen enemy. The gunner (using an overturned chair) may be instructed by the captain that his shot is "too high," "too low," etc., until he gets the proper range.

Red (read).—Have group sit on platform. One player finishes reading a newspaper and passes it to another. This persons passes it on with the information that he has *read* it.

The social chairman should be ready with suggestions for the groups if they need help.

Rainbow Stab.—Against the wall arrange a rainbow effect of colors, cutting the colors out of paper. Or arrange the rainbow colors like a fan, each color narrow at the bottom and spreading to a half foot at the top. Each color has a special number on it from one to seven. Players are blindfolded, provided with a pin stuck through a strip of white cloth, and sent up to stick this on the rainbow or fan. The player is credited with the number of points represented by the color thus stabbed. Each of the seven groups is represented by an equal number of contestants.

Rainbow Relay.—Now select from the seven groups fourteen players to form two rainbow teams. Each team is given seven bits of cloth or ribbon in prismatic combination. Each player is given his color and a pin. A white cloth is hung at the opposite side of the room. The teams line up in the following order: Purple, indigo, blue, green, yellow, orange, and red. Both purples are toeing the mark and at a given signal hop to the white cloth and pin up their colors. They then can race back (not hop) to the starting point and touch off the next player in order, who has moved up to the starting point. The first team to finish its rainbow of colors and get back to the starting point wins.

All the company can now gather about the piano and sing "I'm Always Chasing Rainbows."

For refreshments let every one order by numbers from 1 to 7 without informing them as to what the numbers mean. Three selections are allowed. Thus some one may select 1, 3, and 5, and the waiter would bring a toothpick, an empty glass, and a glass of water, the menu being as follows: 1. Toothpick. 2. Lemonade. 3. Empty glass. 4. Plate. 5. Glass of water. 6. Sandwich. 7. Cake. Of course after the bit of fun all are served lemonade, cake, and sandwiches, or whatever they lacked of this combination.

Additional Suggestions

Rainbow fortunes might be told by placing disks of the different colors on a table and allowing the players blindfolded to touch a color. The colors may be shifted about after the player is blindfolded, so that he won't be sure which spot to touch.

1. Purple means renown and fame,
You will win an honored name.

2. Dark blue's like the rolling sea,
So a traveler you'll be.

3. Since you wisely touch the blue,
You will find a sweetheart true.

4. Now, alas! you've chosen green,
You will never wed, I ween.

5. Yellow means abundant gold,
Thus for you is wealth foretold.

6 (*a*). Orange means this fate's in store,
You'll wed one who's been wed before.

(*b*). Orange means your prospect's bright,
Your wife will let you out at night.

7. Red for you this fate discloses,
You'll wed the first one who proposes.

Another Party Idea.—You may arrange a series of seven stunts, or games, in which all can take part. Award the different colored ribbons for those who are among the first three in the different contests. Thus a hunt will be arranged. The three with the largest number of finds will be awarded a purple ribbon, for instance. Cards are provided, and the colors are pasted on the cards as they are awarded. Or a series of progressive games could be worked out and ribbons be awarded winners instead of punching. the tally cards.

All players completing the rainbow effect on their tally cards might be given some sort of award.

The Cobweb Idea.—Still another way would be to use the old cobweb party idea, winding long pieces of string intricately about the room, over and under chairs, upstairs, etc. Each person takes hold of one end of a string, and the fun begins as they wind here and there, crossing one another, tangling with one another, up the steps, then down again, finally coming to the end of the string just beneath and at one end of the big rainbow, where a prize of some sort is found tied to the string. It may be a small sack of candy or peanuts or some funny little souvenir.

AN EASTER PARTY

Invitations.—Write invitations on butterfly or egg-shaped cards. They may read after this fashion: "An eggs-ellent Easter party has been planned for Friday night by the ——. We are eggs-pecting you to be present. No eggs-cuse will be eggs-cepted. We begin eggs-actly at 8 P.M."

Partners.—Let girls form a line in one room and the boys in another, arranging both lines according to height. Have them march out, meet, and come up double file, so that the tallest become partners, and so on.

Egg Hunt.—Now have an egg hunt, hiding paper eggs about the room. The couple finding the most eggs is declared winner. As prizes you might give them each a "Funny Easter Egg." These may be made in the following manner: Empty an eggshell by pricking a hole in either end and blowing the contents out. Paint a face on it. Make the hole at the small end large enough to allow you to pour in a teaspoonful of small shot. Pour in melted wax on top of the shot. Glue over the top a little round cap of red or blue flannel. No matter how you stand it, it will always right itself.

Easter Hat Show.—Each couple is now furnished with tissue paper, scissors, needle and thread, or paste, etc., and each boy is requested to make an Easter bonnet for his partner to wear. Some wonderful creations will result. When the hats have all been finished, the girls don them and parade before a committee of judges, who decide which is the cleverest creation. The boy who emerges as winner of this contest then appears before the judges, one of whom steps forward and says: "I am going to crush this egg over your hard head, and it isn't hard-boiled either." While saying this he does that very thing. The egg has been emptied of its contents and stuffed with confetti or tissue paper cut in tiny bits. Scent these by spraying with perfumery and cover open end of shell by using a bit of gold paper or a red or green seal. Decorate to suit taste. A similar egg may now be presented to the young man with the compliments of the judges.

Divide the company now into three groups—the Bunnies the Chicks, and the Bad Eggs. Let them engage in the following contests:

Bunny Race.—One contestant will represent each group. They must stoop like "bunnies" and hop to a given goal. Tie a bow of ribbon around the winning "bunny's" neck. If the groups are small in number, every one may have a chance, running one race after another, scoring one point for each winning.

Easter Tenpin.—An equal number of players from each group engage in this contest, using every one present if possible. Little toy chickens are set up as tenpins, and the players bowl with a rubber ball. Have the chicks numbered from 1 to 10 (a smaller number may be used if you find them difficult to get) and far enough apart to keep the scoring from being too heavy. Allow each player three trials. Have a scorer keep track of the scores made.

Decorate the room in yellow and white, which are the Easter colors; yellow as "emblem of the sun and typical of the goodness of God," white as "typical of purity and all things made new."

Another Easter Suggestion

Egg Fortunes.—Put paper eggs of various colors in a box. Players draw without looking.

Draw the red,
Never wed.

Get the blue,
Lovers' true.

Snatch the green,
A husband (wife) that's mean.

If it's the white,
She (he)'s here to-night.

If you choose the brown,
She (he)'s in another town.

If you should pick the pink,
You'll get a peach, I think.

If you should get the yellow,
You (she)'ll get another fellow.

CHAPTER V

MAY PROGRAMS

Indoor Picnic | **Indoor Lawn Party**
Strawberry Social | **Other Suggestions**

INDOOR PICNIC

This social indoor picnic may be used in May or any other month as well.

Decorations.—Use branches of trees. Tie them to pillars or stand them in corners to represent trees. Potted plants will help out. One League holding this social in its Sunday school room hung swings from the balcony, placed several seesaws about the room, covered the floor with leaves, and improvised a spring in one corner by making a mound of leaves around a bucket of clear, cold water. Here the picnickers could come for a drink. A lemonade stand where lemonade and cake are served is also a possibility.

The picnic is a joint affair for the pupils of Sleepy Hollow and Podunk Sunday Schools. Superintendents have been appointed for these wide-awake schools, and every one is assigned to one group or the other.

As one of the big features on such occasions is the contest between the two schools for supremacy in certain events, so the contest idea may feature in the evening's program.

Merry-Go-Round

First let everybody take a ride on the merry-go-round. Form a big circle and play the kindergarten game "Luby

Loo." For those who don't know this game the following brief explanation is necessary. The players all sing, suiting action to the words:

"I put my right foot in,
I put my right foot out,
I give my foot a shake, shake, shake,
And turn myself about."

Chorus (all skip about in circle, taking holds of hands):

"Here we go, Luby Loo,
Here we go, Luby light,
Here we go, Luby Loo,
On a Saturday night."

Then "I put my left foot in," etc.

"I put my right hand in," etc.
"I put my left hand in," etc.
"I put my head in," etc.
"I put my body in," etc.

(All march toward the center, then back on last verse.)

Crisscross Bean Bag

Line up at least ten contestants from each side, with contestants alternating down the lines which face one another. Thus down one line will be first a Podunkite, then a Sleepy Hollowite, and so on down the line. The line facing them will have first a Sleepy Hollowite, then a Podunkite, and so on. Five white bean bags are given to the captain of one side, standing at the head of one line, and five red or blue bean bags to the captain standing at the head of the other line. At a given signal the captains start the bean bags one at a time down the line in zigzag fashion. That is, he tosses it to No. 2 in the line opposite him, No. 2

tosses it across to No. 3, and so on. The first team getting all its bean bags back to its captain is given five points. Should a player throw to a player on the opposing team, or should he drop the bean bag, one point is credited to the opposing team for each error.

Pictures

One of the features of most big picnics is the picture man who makes 'em while you wait. Stretch a sheet over a doorway. Place a lighted candle or arrange your lights so that a clear-cut shadow will show on the screen when a person stands back of it. Each Sunday school will take turn about guessing the names of the persons whose shadows show on the screen. First, one school will have the shadows of all its members shown, one at a time. Then the other school exchanges places with them. The school guessing the most correctly wins.

Baseball Game

Nine players represent each team. Those "at the bat" take places on the bench. The team in the field takes regular positions, and the game is played as described in "Baseball Buzz."

Quoits

A match game of quoits may be played with a ringtoss set. Two players could represent each Sunday school. Twenty-one points is out.

Fishing

Let all the girls gather in one room, all the boys in another. Put a screen across the door between and let the boys fish for partners. A boy steps up toward the screen with fishing pole and line. He tosses the line over the screen, and some girl takes hold of it and thus becomes his partner for "eats." Thus each boy goes fishing for a partner.

Eats

The girls have prepared sandwiches, pickles, etc., and now all the company become seated in a large circle on the floor, the food being served out before them picnic fashion. Ice cream could be served in cones from a booth.

Songs

Close the evening's program with the singing of some familiar songs.

STRAWBERRY SOCIAL

A strawberry social or festival always makes a strong appeal. One we attended at one time had the following most entertaining program:

They had advertised as a special feature "A Mysterious Male Quartet." No one but the members of the committee were "in" on it. At the proper time four boys from the group entered in costumes of the Gay Nineties and began to sing such old familiar songs as "Sweet Adeline," "After the Ball," and "My Wild Irish Rose." The sounds actually came from a phonograph behind the scenes, and the boys silently pretended to do the singing with extravagant gestures. Having rehearsed thoroughly with the records, each one moved his lips along with the specific voice he represented, and stepped forward for his "solo" part when his cue came. This surprise sent the crowd into gales of laughter and put everyone in a good frame of mind to enjoy the rest of the evening's program.

We next *Matched for Partners.* Pictures of men had been cut in two and passed around, half to the girls and half to the boys. These pictures had been cut out of fashion books gotten from a men's clothing shop.

The couples thus formed engaged now in a *Man Completer Game.* Paper and pencil were given to each couple, with a list of the following questions:

1. The man to be avoided? Mansion.
2. The traveling man? Mango.
3. The untruthful man? Manly.
4. The man for the violent criminal? Manacle.
5. The musical man? Mandolin.
6. The gossiping man? Mantel.
7. The stable man? Manger.
8. The court man? Mandamus.
9. The dye man? Human.
10. The physician? Manicure.
11. The literary man? Manuscript.
12. The married man? Herman.
13. The many-sided man? Manifold.
14. The oarsman? Roman.
15. The Hebrew man of the desert? Manna.
16. The Chinese man? Mandarin.
17. The man with many engagements? Mandate.
18. The small man? Manikin.
19. The book man to whom we often go for help? Manual.
20. The butcher man? Manslaughter.

The couple winning in this contest were invited to the platform. Two dishes of ice cream and strawberries and two spoons were placed on a small table. They were invited to sit on opposite sides of the table and feed one another ice cream and strawberries in full view of the crowd. Both entered into the spirit of the thing and much merriment resulted.

Banana Ensemble.—As a closing feature of the evening's

fun four teams of three men each took their places on the platform. Bananas were passed out. At a given signal the first man on each team began peeling and then eating his banana. As soon as he finished No. 2 began. The first team to consume the bananas in this fashion was declared winner.

Strawberries, ice cream, and cake were served as refreshments.

OTHER MAY SUGGESTIONS

An indoor lawn party would make a jolly occasion. Decorate with plants, benches, porch chairs, Japanese lanterns, etc. Have the young people bring their banjos, ukuleles, and guitars. Sing popular songs and League "pep" songs. Let everything be done in informal style, but don't allow things to drag. Play "Slang," "Truth," "Throwing the Handkerchief," and any other games you think desirable. Light some candles and have a marshmallow roast. The marshmallows could be held over the flame on sharp-pointed sticks. Serve lemonade, colored with a few cupfuls of strawberry juice, and cake.

Have a *May-Time Party* and play a lot of rollicking games. For ages the first day of May has been one of frolic. May games were played back in the Middle Ages.

The Snow Frolic described for December can be easily adapted to this month, putting fortunes on the strings around the snowman's neck instead of presents.

CHAPTER VI

JUNE PROGRAMS

A FLOWER SOCIAL

Decorate with a profusion of flowers and plants. Make the room as attractive as possible. Write the invitations on pansies that have been cut out of paper and painted by the Social Committee. Ask each person to wear his birth month flower. Give each person on entering a rose to wear. Let these be pinned on by girls wearing garlands of flowers hung about the neck and a wreath of flowers on the head.

Flower Hunt.—Write names of birth month flowers on slips, at least twenty for each month. Hide these about the room. Tell the players to hunt, but to pick up only those of their own month. For instance, one born in June could collect only "roses." The hunters must not assist one another in making discoveries of flowers. A short time is allowed for the hunt, when the social chairman or leader should blow a horn for the return of the hunters. Flowers are counted, and the winning boy and girl may be given an additional rose each.

Birth Month Flowers.—January, snowdrop; February, primrose; March, violet; April, daisy; May, hawthorn; June, rose; July, poppy; August, water lily; September, morning-glory or goldenrod; October, hop vine or aster; November, chrysanthemum; December, holly.

A Floral Love Story.—Now pass out paper and pencils

and let the players answer the following questions with the names of flowers:

1. Her name and the color of her hair? Marigold.
2. Her brother's name, and what he wrote it with? Jonquil.
3. Her brother's favorite musical instrument? Trumpet.
4. With what did his father punish him when he made too much noise with it? Goldenrod.
5. What did the boy do? Balsam.
6. At what time did his father awaken him? Four-o'clock.
7. What did he say to him? Johnny-jump-up.
8. What office did father hold in the church? Elder.
9. What did she call her lover? Sweet William.
10. What, being single, did he often lose? Bachelor's button.
11. What did he do when he proposed? Aster.
12. What did he lay at her feet? Bleeding heart.
13. What did she give him in return? Heartsease.
14. What flower did he cultivate? Tulips.
15. To whom did she refer him? Poppy.
16. Who married them? Jack-in-the-pulpit.
17. When he went away, what did she say to him? Forget-me-not.
18. With what did she punish her children? Lady's slipper.
19. What hallowed their last days? Sweet peas.

Another Writing Contest

1. What flower gives the time? Four-o'clock.
2. What flower is an incessant traveler? Wandering Jew.
3. What flower illumines? Morning-glory.

4. What flower is festive? Hop.

5. What flower is a popular man with the ladies? Sweet William.

6. What flower is religious? Jack-in-the-pulpit.

7. What flower has the names of two girls? Rosemary.

Daisy Fortune Teller.—Make several different bunches of paper daisies. These may be presided over by the Flower Queen, who directs that each player shall come forward and pull one leaf off of one daisy in each set. The words of the fortune are written with ink on the underside of the petals. The first set tells the seeker's chief virtue, the next tells the greatest fault, the third the future occupation, and the fourth some future fate.

Flower Garden.—Give each player the name of some flower. Have them sit in a circle with one player standing in the center. He may say: "I enter the flower garden, and I want a rose and a lily." Players with those names must immediately change seats, while the center player endeavors to get one of the vacated seats. When he succeeds the player losing out must take his place in the center. When the center player announces a "windstorm" all flowers must change seats, and in the general mix-up the player standing may endeavor to get a chair.

A Rose Relay Race might be worked out, using the Shuttle Relay as a basis, the runners carrying a rose from one side of the course to the other. Or the Weaver's Relay might be used, the first player carrying the rose, delivering it to the player to the right of his original position as he finishes. This player carries the rose as he weaves in and out and then passes it to the player to his right until the entire group has run and the rose has been returned to the first player to run. Immediately he receives it he holds it high above his head so that the judges may see that his team has finished.

A Sunflower Song Show may also be worked out for the entertainment of your crowd. Each one of those who takes part in this will be fitted out with a stiff, wide, yellow petal collar giving the effect of a large sunflower. This may be fashioned by cutting the collar out of stiff cardboard and covering the petals with yellow cloth or paper. Or all participants may stick their heads through an opening in a long strip of cloth. Around each opening has been fashioned a large sunflower, either by painting or by sewing yellow petals on the cloth. Songs may be sung in this manner and jokes pulled off on persons present. "My Wild Irish Rose," "The Rose of No Man's Land," "You Wore a Tulip," "The Last Rose of Summer," and any songs of this sort will fit in appropriately.

A FLAG PARTY

June 14 is Flag Day, making a flag party appropriate for that day. The social might be held on a large porch or on the lawn. When held out of doors, Japanese lanterns should be added to the decorating scheme. Have an abundance of flags everywhere.

Stars

Begin your program by having every one sing "The Star-Spangled Banner." Then introduce some special musical numbers and readings appropriate for such an occasion. The "stars" will shine in these features. A suggested program follows:

Reading: "Your Flag and My Flag." Wilbur Nesbit.

Solo: "Flag of My Heart." Werrenrath. (Victor Record.)

Song: "Battle Hymn of the Republic." (Make the congregational singing a feature of the program.)

Reading: "The Name of Old Glory." (James Whitcomb Riley.)

Stunt: "How the Flag Was Made."

Two soldiers on guard duty pass each other. "Say, we ain't got no flag," says one of them. "Gee, ain't it fierce?" is the reply. "I'll see George about it." One soldier passes off the scene, and Gen. George Washington appears. Guard goes through burlesque salute and then says: "Say, George, we ain't got no flag." "Gee, ain't it fierce?" replies George. "I'd better see Betsy about it." The next scene shows George calling on Betsy Ross. "Betsy, we ain't got no flag." "I know, George. Ain't it fierce? I think I'll have to make one." Betsy turns her back to the audience and pretends to be sewing a flag. Then she turns with the completed flag and waves it.

Stripes

Divide the party into two sides, the Reds and the Whites. Put on the Flag Relay as suggested in the chapter for February. Let the two groups engage in the flag contest, all the persons in each group working together on the answers to the questions asked.

Flag Contest

1. A stone or a flower? Flag.
2. A fanatic who scourges himself? Flagellant.
3. A musical instrument? Flageolet.
4. The sort of spirit some of our members show? Flagging.
5. A grossly wicked flag? Flagitious.
6. A railroad flag? Flagman.
7. A flag popular with anti-prohibitionists? Flagon.
8. A notorious flag? Flagrant.
9. A naval flag? Flagship.
10. A tall flag? Flagstaff or flagpole.

Some Patriotic Victrola Records

"Taps" (musical setting by Pasternock). Schumann-Heink.

"My Own United States." Dixon and male quartet.

"We'll Never Let the Old Flag Fall." Hamilton.

"American War Songs." Victor mixed chorus.

"Star-Spangled Banner." John McCormick.

CHAPTER VII

JULY PROGRAMS

A PATRIOTIC PARTY

Here's a party that can be appropriately given on July 4, Flag Day, or Washington's birthday.

Singsong

Have a rousing singsong, using many of the songs made popular during the war, such as "Keep the Home Fires Burning," "Over There," "There's a Long, Long Trail," "Long Boy," "Round Her Neck She Wore a Yellow Ribbon," etc. You might also use some of the familiar home songs and hymns. Close the singsong with the singing of "The Star-Spangled Banner," every one standing, of course.

Progressive Conversation

Form two circles, with the girls on the inner circle and the boys on the outer one. Let the circles march in opposite directions to martial music. When the music stops, the marchers stop and face one another. A leader announces the first topic for conversation, allows them a short time to talk, then taps a bell. Each boy moves up one partner, another topic is announced, and so on. The leader should keep the movement lively by tapping the bell at short intervals, compelling a change of partners. The following subjects may be discussed:

1. Loyalty
2. America the Beautiful
3. National Unity
4. Duty to Country
5. Our Democratic Heritage
6. Freedom for All
7. Law and Order
8. In God We Trust
9. Beneath Old Glory
10. E Pluribus Unum
11. Revolutionary Days
12. Truth and Justice
13. Yankee Doodle

You will note that this list of topics makes an acrostic, spelling "Land of Liberty." Ask if any one has discovered, during the game, the big topic for the whole evening. (Other names may be spelled in like manner, as above.)

Ringing Liberty Bell

Divide the company into three groups—the Reds, the Whites, and the Blues. Make a heavy cardboard bell of several thicknesses of cardboard. Cut a hole in the center of it some four inches in diameter. Hang this bell in a doorway, tying it with heavy strings at the top and on either side, holding it in place so it will not swing back and forth. Immediately behind the hole in the bell and several inches back of it hangs a small bell. The idea is for players to stand some ten or more feet away and toss a tennis or small rubber ball through the hole, causing the bell to ring. Each player gets one try, and points are kept, the side totaling the greatest score winning.

Reading

Have some one give James Whitcomb Riley's "Old Glory" or "Your Flag and My Flag" as a reading, or any other patriotic number.

Shuttle Flag Relay

Have the three groups represented in this race by teams of ten members each. Mark out the course and line up the teams in rows, half of each team being lined up on one side of the course and half on the other. Hand a small flag to the leader of each team. At a given signal three leaders run to the opposite side of the course, handing the flag to the first runner in line as he reaches the line. This runner immediately rushes to the opposite side, handing it to No. 2 in the line just opposite, No. 2 having moved up to the starting point in the meantime, and so on. The team all of whose runners carry the flag across the course in quickest time wins.

Refreshments

Ice cream or hot chocolate and star-shaped cakes may be served. Also serve red, white, and blue mints.

Decorations

Let there be a profusion of the national colors, flags, etc. Stick a potato full of tiny flags and hang it from the doorsill.

INTRODUCING GEORGE AND MRS. WASHINGTON

Here's a stunt that's full of fun. Put all the players out of the room and bring them in one at a time to meet the distinguished guests. One player acts as go-between, bringing the guests in and introducing them. George and Martha stand over in one corner. It is not necessary that they be in costume. The guest is brought forward and introduced with much to-do to Gen. George Washington, who expresses his pleasure as he shakes hands with the guest. The General now very graciously requests that the guest meet Mrs. Washington. This time when the victim holds out his hand to shake hands as Mrs. Washington extends hers, the General steps forward and shakes Mrs. Washington's hand, leaving the guest with hand extended and feeling very foolish.

OTHER JULY SUGGESTIONS

"Eats"

Chocolates done up in red tissue paper to look like torpedoes. Stick candy wrapped in red tissue paper to represent firecrackers. Stick tiny flag in individual cakes or in the ice cream. Wrap sandwiches in white tissue paper and tie with red, white, and blue striped ribbon. Serve, red, white, and blue stick candy, which may be obtained at any up-to-date confectioner's.

Red, White, and Blue Contest

Arrange your company in couples. Give out papers, having written at the top "Red, White, and Blue," each color being spaced off and a line drawn down the entire length of the paper, thus giving three columns. The partners work together on the contest. The couples contest to see which can make the largest list of red, white, and blue articles or things. The boys write, and the girls dictate. The boys are not allowed to do any suggesting, nor can they write anything except as the girls dictate. Only absolutely red articles may go in the red column, only white in the white column, only blue in the blue column. Red—blood, lips. White, snow, sugar. Blue—sky, violet.

Artists' Demonstration

Select five persons to be artists for the crowd. Give each a slip of paper, with instructions to go to the blackboard and draw with chalk the historical event written on the paper. Each in turn steps up and draws the scene named. The first person guessing what is represented each time may get some sort of recognition. For instance, if the red, white, and blue party is put on, a red ribbon may be pasted on the card of the player. These are some of the subjects to be guessed:

1. "Washington Crossing the Delaware."
2. "Landing of the Pilgrims."
3. "The Midnight Ride of Paul Revere."
4. "Battle of the Monitor and the Merrimac."
5. "Betsy Ross Making the First American Flag."
6. "George Washington and the Cherry Tree."

Red, White, and Blue Party

Use the Red, White, and Blue Contest, the Artists' Demonstration, and the Flag Contest described in the Flag Party for June. Allow each person of the first five couples in the Red, White, and Blue Contest to have a blue ribbon pasted on tally card. Each one who guesses correctly before the others in the Artists' Demonstration gets a red ribbon pasted on the card, and the first three couples in the Flag Contest, working that by couples, a white ribbon.

Let all those completing the trinity of colors draw for a prize. Contests may also be engaged in by dividing the party into three groups, the Reds, the Whites, and the Blues.

A Columbia Party

Decorate with flags, bunting, and Japanese lanterns. Have transparencies showing the dates 1776 and the present year. These can easily be made by using a little pasteboard and tissue paper and should appear just outside the door. Uncle Sam and Columbia will receive the guests. Ask the girls to come dressed in crêpe paper patriotic costumes. These can be made by sewing the crêpe paper on old dresses. Give a prize for the most clever creation.

Bubble Tennis

For a lawn party or Fourth-of-July picnic a game of bubble tennis could be played. The company is divided into two sides or into as many groups as the size of the crowd demands. Not more than ten on a side should contest at a time. The girls are to blow bubbles, and the boys are to endeavor to blow or fan them over the net, at the same time trying to keep the opposing side from sending them over. The side getting the most bubbles over the net wins, of course.

CHAPTER VIII

AUGUST PROGRAMS

Gypsy Party
Watermelon Feast
A Freeze-Up Party
A Garden Party
Circle Croquet
Moonlight Picnic

GYPSY PARTY

An announcement of a gypsy party ought to arouse considerable interest, especially if you link it up with the idea of a lawn party or, better, of a hike to some near-by park or outdoor beauty spot. Ask all the girls to come dressed in all sorts of gay-colored costumes—the velvet bodice when obtainable—with hair loose or braided down the back. Yellow and red cheesecloth or a brilliant gingham would solve the dress problem. Ask the boys to come in old clothes, with bandana handkerchief about the neck instead of the stiff white collar. They may wear coats or not, at their pleasure. As it seems to be the style to wear shirts of various "loud" hues, young men blessed with pink or light blue or green shirts or any of the present-day "loud" creations would do well to doff the coat and wear a vest instead.

A gypsy kettle on a tripod, ought to be part of the equipment. Three poles and a bit of wire will make the tripod. And of course you ought to have a camp fire. Lemonade might be served from the kettle. Or you might make effective use of it by filling it with water, building a good fire under it, dropping in wieners, and having "hot dogs'' and rolls. Lots of marshmallows should be taken along so you can have a marshmallow roast. For this you cut a twig, point it, stick your marshmallow on the end, and hold it in the flame until it is browned a bit, making it a delicious confection. A wiener roast is another possibility.

It would be fun if you could take along some one who understands a little of palmistry and set up a fortune-telling tent. Or seat the crowd about on the ground and have them seat themselves one at a time before the ''gypsy fortune teller'' to learn the fate in store for them.

Kidnaper

Play ''Kidnaper,'' which is an adaptation of ''Rabbit,'' described elsewhere. One player is ''kidnaper,'' and another is the ''child.'' The rest of the players form in groups of four, three joining hands forming the ''home'' and the fourth standing inside the home thus formed. The kidnaper starts after the child, who dodges in and out among the other groups. To save himself the child may take refuge in one of the homes by dodging in under the arms of the players. Immediately the player occupying that home must vacate, dodging out on the other side and becoming the child, fleeing from the kidnaper. The former child takes the place of one of the players forming the home, that player taking the center of the group. When a child is captured or tagged, he becomes kidnaper, and the former kidnaper takes the place of some player forming a home, that player becoming the child.

Instead of the wiener plans a picnic lunch might be served. Of course, if the hike idea is adopted, you should select a moonlight night for your frolic.

Watermelon Feast

Luscious watermelon has an appeal all its own. The feast may be arranged as a lawn affair, or a long auto truck ride may be taken out into the country. We know of an active group of young people who have a glorious time each year using the latter plan. They ride out to a country home, singing, laughing, joking, and bubbling over with the exuberance of youth. There they play games, such as drop the handkerchief, for instance, on the lawn, gather around the piano and sing, etc. The climax of the evening's fun is the cutting and serving of the watermelons they have carried with them. A watermelon-eating contest may be put on, with the boys as contestants. They'll be in it up to their ears, and it will be lots of fun.

A Freeze-Up Party

This should be held on the lawn or on the porch of some one's home. Cover all the porch chairs and benches with white. Drop bunches of cotton on the branches of the plants and bushes, or cover them with papers and white cloths, as if to protect them from the frost. All decorations are white. Fines may be assessed on all speaking of hot weather, or forfeits required of them. The ice-guessing contest outlined in the "Snow Frolic" for December may be used. Or you might use this one, bringing in the "freezer" idea:

1. What the cold weather is liable to do for you. Freesia (freeze ya).
2. A mighty cold stone. Freestone (freeze stone).
3. A cold proposition when it comes to ornamenting a wall. Frieze.
4. A cold Teutonic country. Friesland.
5. How a Frenchman in this country would describe a playful, gamboling spirit. Frisky (freeskee).

Play games with the "freeze-out" idea. For instance, play "Buzz," having players making mistakes drop out; or play "Going to Jerusalem," though you may call it "Going to Friesland or to Freeze-Out Town." "The Laughing Handkerchief," described in connection with the Pollyanna Social, would also make a good "freeze-out" game. For refreshments serve pear and pineapple salad with whipped cream, iced tea, and frosted cake.

A Garden Party

This could be made an attractive outdoor social function for August. Japanese lanterns, palms, and flowers are needed to add to the festive appearance. Ask the young people to bring their "ukes," banjos, and guitars. Encourage informal group singing and playing. If a male quartet is available, it would add materially to the evening's entertainment. Or if you haven't an organized quartet, a little encouragement to some of the young people who like to get together occasionally and "harmonize" some would help. Readings, solo-singing to ukelele accompaniment, stringed-instrument selections, and games would make a delightful evening of fun. Serve sandwiches, salted peanuts, and iced grape juice, iced tea, or frappé.

Circle Croquet or Golf

Dig twelve holes in a circle and one in the center. Use a ball that is golf size or an ordinary croquet ball. The player wins who can get around in the least number of strokes, beginning at the center, driving to one of the circle holes, and then on around the circle and back to the center, always "holing" the ball before proceeding. Sides may be chosen and scores kept to determine which is the winning side, or teams of thirteen each may contest, each player being assigned a hole. The center player starts the ball rolling toward player No. 1. No. 1 must endeavor to "hole" the ball from where it stops. As soon as No. 1 has "holed" it he takes it out and drives to No. 2, and so on around and back to center. Of course if any player "holes" it in one stroke as he drives it to his team-mate, so much the better. This game could be used to advantage at a picnic or outing.

Moonlight Picnic

I got in touch with different men of our congregation who had machines and asked them to kindly lend them to us, which they gladly did. I asked them to promise to keep it a secret. So on the night of our business meeting, when the meeting was turned over to me, I had the lights all turned out and had the men who drove the machines to come in with toy guns and flashlights and make every one throw up his hands. Then I called off names, having prearranged them for different groups to go in different machines, so the crowds that went together were people who usually grouped together, thus making it more congenial. They were led out to the sidewalk, without knowing anything of what was going to take place, and when every one was in we started off. We went to one of our parks. There we had a spot arranged with Japanese lanterns. We let everybody out there and then played old-time games and served refreshments. Every one who attended this affair pronounced it a great success. Of course this party was held in warm weather.—*Prize stunt, Nettie Zurborg, Covington, Ky.*

CHAPTER IX

SEPTEMBER PROGRAMS

AN OLD-TIME SCHOOL PARTY

It would be lots of fun to have an old-time school party. Ask the girls to dress as schoolgirls (middie blouses or gingham dresses), and the boys might wear Buster Brown collars and big bow ties. Some might even be brave enough to wear knee trousers. Let your invitations read:

"Now come, ye children, hale and hearty,
To our old-time school party.
School begins on the stroke of eight.
Date, ——, now don't be late.
Readin', 'ritin', and 'rithmetic,
Jography to make you sick;
A spellin' bee and loads of fun.
The (name organization) wants you to come.
If you do, you'll sure be glad;
Play hookey, and you'll get in bad.
So come, ye children, hale and hearty,
To our old-time school party."

The schoolma'am, who has been previously appointed, comes attired for the occasion. Tally cards are handed the guests as they arrive. They may be made to represent a book cover, and at the bottom may be written:

"School days, school days,
Dear old golden-rule days."

The teacher rings the bell, and school opens. The girls have assembled in one room, the boys in another. Immediately on the ringing of the bell the piano strikes up "Tipperary," "Over There," or some other good popular tune, and the children march in from opposite directions, the two lines meeting and then marching around the room two by two. Thus they are matched up as partners for the first game. The children march around and take their places at the different tables. Standing at the tables, they sing the chorus of "School Days."

1. *Progressive Arithmetic.*—The teacher now announces that the first subject will be "Progressive Arithmetic." Each table has been covered with paper on which are drawn four circles, reaching to the outer edge of the table. The intervening spaces are numbered 30, 35, 40, and the outer rim 50. A spool top is on each table. These can be easily made by cutting a spool in two and sharpening the cylindrical part to a point. Into the top fit a small stick of wood, protruding at the top end enough to furnish sufficient grip for the spin and at the lower end protruding enough to furnish a suitable point. Each one at the table is allowed three spins—this always being done from the center. The space on which the top rests after spinning is counted for the spinner. Totals are noted on tally cards. Partners having the highest total move to the next table, having tally card punched. At the end the girl and the boy having the highest total receive each an extra punch.

2. *Reading.*—The teacher calls up a few "star" pupils and hands out a list of tongue twisters to be read rapidly. If she thinks it best, she may line up the entire class and

make each one read, urging them to greater speed and sending them to the foot for making mistakes. Here are a few:

(1) Two toads teetotally trying to trot to Trixburg.
(2) Five fantastic Frenchmen fanning five fainting females.
(3) Six slippery snakes sliding slowly southward.
(4) Nine nautical Norwegians nearing neighboring Norway.
(5) Ten tiny toddling tots trying to train their tongues to trill.
(6) A bitter biting bittern
Bit a better brother bittern;
And the bitter better bittern bit the bitter biter back.
And the bitter bittern, bitten
By the better bitten bittern,
Said: "I'm a bitter biter bit, alack!"

3. *Geography.*—Pupils are told to gather at same tables as for the arithmetic lesson. On each table is a heap of slips of paper on which are written letters of the alphabet, all face down. Each player in turn turns up a letter. The first at each table to call out the name of a city, river, mountain, etc., beginning with that letter, as directed by the teacher, takes up the slip. For instance, the teacher calls "rivers." At one table "O" happens to be turned up, and some one shouts "Ohio" and takes up the slip. The boy and the girl with the largest number of slips after one round pass to the next table, having tally cards punched for geography, putting the slips back on the table. If the crowd is large, and this threatens to consume too much time, have the leaders at each table gather about one table to decide the "star" pupil in geography.

4. *Recess.*—The teacher rings the bell for recess. Some one has been appointed beforehand to start recess games. Play simple children's games, such as "Sugar-Loaf Town," "Farmer's in the Dell," etc. The appearance of two or three lunch men, dressed in white caps, coats, and aprons and carrying trays of sandwiches, is the signal for breaking

up the games. The tables have been moved out of the room and an old-fashioned well placed in the center. This well can be easily made by using a large dry goods box and covering it with white cheesecloth. Down inside is placed a bucket of ice-cold lemonade. Two girls take charge of the well and serve lemonade to all who come to the well. The lunch men appear a second time bearing trays of marshmallows.

5. The bell rings, and recess is over. A *Spelling Bee* is to be the big feature following recess. Divide the crowd into two sides. You may have a regular spelling bee or one in which the contestants must spell the words backward, or you may hang two sets of letters on the individuals of the two sides and call out a word. The first side to spell the word by getting into proper position in front of their line scores a point. This may be continued until an agreed number of words have been spelled.

One of the school trustees now steps forward and presents prizes to the brightest boys and girls in the various studies. These should be inexpensive. Cardboard tags bearing suitable inscription, for instance, may serve as medal awards to prize winners.

A List of Tongue Twisters

1. Four fat friars fanning flickering flames.
2. She sells sea shells by the seashore.
3. Two timid toads trying to trot to Tarrytown.
4. Three terrible, thumping tigers tickling trout.
5. Five frivolous foreigners fleeing from fabulous snipe.
6. Seven serious Southerners setting sail for Switzerland.
7. Six Scottish soldiers successfully shooting snipe.
8. Eight eager emigrants earnestly examining elements.
9. Nine nimble noblemen nibbling nuts.

10. Ten tremendous tomtits twittering on the tops of three tall trees.

11. Eleven enormous elephants elegantly eating Easter eggs.

12. Twelve tired tailors thoughtfully twisting twine.

13. Nine floating fly boats full of fruits and flowers.

14. Seven suffering saints supping soup slowly.

15. Peter Piper picked a peck of pickled peppers.

16. How much wood would a woodchuck chuck if a woodchuck would chuck wood?

17. How much dew would a dewdrop drop if a dewdrop could drop dew?

18. How many shoes would the sunshine shine if the sunshine could shine shoes?

19. There was a young fisher named Fischer,
Who fished for a fish in a fissure.
The fish with a grin
Pulled the fisherman in,
And they're fishing the fissure for Fischer.

20. Sister Susie's sewing shirts for soldiers.

21. "A glowing gleam growing green."

22. The black breeze blighted the bright blossoms.

23. Flesh of fresh flying fish.

24. Six thick thistle sticks.

25. Two toads tried to trot to Tedbury.

26. Give Grimes Jim's great gilt gig whip.

27. Slick, strong Stephen Stringer snared six slick, sickly, silky snakes.

28. She stood at the gate waiting for slick, strong Stephen Stringer, who snared six slick, sickly, silky snakes.

A "POP" SOCIAL

Invitation

Surely we won't need a cop
To make you come to our "pop."
"Pop" Social——,
Friday eve, September 24.
"Better come, old top."

As each one arrives hand him an ear of pop corn and a wooden plate. Let him shell the corn, count the grains, remembering the count, putting it down on a slip of paper, and turning it in to the social chairman. He then pours the contents of his plate into a large receptacle designated for that purpose. When all have poured their corn into this receptacle, each person makes a guess as to the total number of grains, the one coming nearest to the correct number getting a prize. These guesses are written on slips of paper with the name of the guessers and turned in to the social chairman. The chairman in the meantime has added together all the individual slips first handed in, thus obtaining the correct total.

Popping for Partners.—Have the girls form a large circle. Bring the men in one at a time. Blindfold this one. Place the blindfolded player in the center of the circle and have the girls skip about him until he shouts "Pop," when they must all stop. He then points, and the girl toward whom he points becomes his partner.

Popping Corn.—The men are now provided with poppers and proceed to pop the corn that has been shelled. After a large enough quantity has been popped, each one is given a needle and thread and a piece of ribbon or cloth strip about half an inch wide. These latter should be of a variety of colors. The girls make watch chains for the boys, and the boys necklaces for the girls, sewing the grains on the ribbons or strips of cloth.

A Popping Contest.—Give out paper and pencil to each couple and let them work together on the following popping contest (words having "pop" in them):

1. A Roman Catholic pop? Popery.
2. A talkative pop? Popin-jay.
3. A tree pop? Poplar.
4. A pop in fabric? Poplin.
5. A flower pop? Poppy.
6. The pop of the common people? Populace.
7. An uncertain but much-sought pop? Popularity.
8. A political pop of some few years back? Populist.
9. A thickly inhabited pop? Populous.
10. A toy pop? Popgun.
11. The pride of large cities? Population.

Popping the Question.—Have each boy write a proposal of marriage and let the girls vote by ballot as to the most clever production. Or have the boys "pop" the question as in "Progressive Proposal." Conduct it after this manner: Each boy is allowed only a limited time to "pop" the question, a bell ringing to stop proceedings and to notify him to move on to the next girl. The girls endeavor to keep the boys from coming to a definite proposal by all sorts of diverting remarks and by turning to the discussion to other channels. The boys are not permitted to propose abruptly, but must preface the proposal by introductory remarks such as would be common. When a boy does succeed in "getting over" his proposal before the bell rings, the girl must give him a grain of pop corn to indicate the fact. Therefore each girl has a supply of pop corn at hand. The boy finishing up with the most grains of corn won in this manner is recognized as "champion popper."

In leap year the popping may be done by the girls.

Refreshments.—Pop corn balls or salted and buttered pop corn and apples.

Decorate with white and red ears of corn.

HIKES AND WIENER OR MARSHMALLOW ROASTS

September is a fine month for hikes and wiener roasts. You must be careful about the distance to be covered in your hikes. "Stag" hikes don't require so much care. Boys are more rugged and can enjoy a hike that would simply wear some girls out. So make your hikes reasonable. Pick out a suitable destination both with regard to distance and natural beauty. Let the boys "tote the footin's" to build a fire and have a good time roasting wieners or marshmallows. Sing songs as you hike along. Every soldier will tell you how singing helped him to forget the discomforts of a long hike or added joy to a short one. The writer has in mind two such incidents that will always appeal to him as times when the joy tide was high in his soul.

A NEW HIKING SUGGESTION

Recently we had a very successful affair in the shape of a trailing party. The Leaguers met at the church and were divided into two parties. The first party proceeded twenty minutes ahead of the second and dropped a trail —white confetti (or paper cut into small bits). The trail led down by an old pond, where we built a fire, cooked "hot dog," roasted potatoes and marshmallows, played games, etc.—*Miss Beryl W. Hundley.*

CHAPTER X

OCTOBER PROGRAMS

HALLOWE'EN PARTY

Next Friday on Hallowe'en
At Oaklawn Church I will be seen.
If you want to know your future fate,
Be there when the clock strikes eight.
Great mysteries I will unfold;
Your future mate you may behold;
I'll stew for you some witch's brew.
So come and bring a friend or two.

Decorations make things interesting from the beginning. With curtains and screens make long, narrow, dimly lighted passages to caves made of brush piled together and covered with leaves. One of these, Mystery Hall, passes a number of Sunday school classrooms in which old witches have been placed who make gruesome noises. Make huge jack-o'-lanterns of old witches riding brooms and swing them on a drop with a red light in the center of some of the classrooms. They look as if they are flying through the air. Mystery Hall parties are formed and are led by witches. Have the social parlors very dimly lighted, with an old spook wrapped in a sheet, holding a white kid glove stuffed with meal and soaked in ice water, to receive the guests. In front of one of the caves have an old witch telling fortunes. (Get the best palmist you can find.) Let another hall lead to Mystery Cave, in which witches serve from a menu (menus can be very artistically made and decorated) sidewalk slippers (bananas), fountain of youth (water), staff of life (bread), falling tears (onion), etc. Another hall leads to a cave or hut of an old witch who is serving the "witch's brew" from an iron pot swung from three sticks over a fire (made of red lights and crêpe paper). Punch may be served for the brew. Bobbing and biting of apples may be kept going on in other caves.

An interesting Hallowe'en game: Let some one start making up a ghost story with two or three sentences and every one in turn add two or three more lines (any one talking out of time pays a forfeit).—*Opal Wallace, Dallas, Texas.*

HALLOWE'EN SOCIAL

One organization put on a Hallowe'en Social that was voted a success by those who attended. The affair was held in the Sunday school room. Jack-o'-lanterns faced one from every angle in the big room. The electric light globes about the room were covered with orange crêpe (noninflammable) paper, eyes, nose, and mouth of black paper being pasted on them. Two pumpkins for decoration were made by stuffing orange crêpe paper with newspaper and shaping like a pumpkin. Pumpkin heads were cut out of paper, pasted on black paper curtains, and hung about the room. On the platform a fortune teller's booth was built out of cornstalks and branches of autumn trees. Inside in the glow of a red light sat the fortune teller, who read the palms of those young people who presented themselves. A tripod and caldron occupied the center of the room, the floor beneath it being covered with cornstalks and apples. "Witch's brew" (lemonade or frappé) was found in the caldron. The guests helped themselves to the apples.

A ghost in the hall silently directed every one upstairs. At the top of the steps another ghost motioned them to a place where they could leave their wraps. They were then directed to walk around the balcony and enter the Sunday school room from steps on the other side.

On the way around they had all sorts of "scary" experiences. At one place "Tige," a boy dressed up as a dog, suddenly jumped out at them barking and growling. The young man who took this part had a suit made out of brown crêpe paper, the same being sewed on an old suit of clothes. A short tail was made by wrapping cloth around a piece of wire and covering the whole thing with brown paper. A brown hood and false dog face completed his equipment, except that a small dog house had been improvised. "Tige" proved one of the "hits" of the evening.

Further on an electric fan blew tissue paper streamers suddenly into the faces of the guests. Ghosts patrolled the balcony to prevent any excitable one from toppling over to the floor below in his fright.

Just inside the door that led downstairs, in a dark passageway, stood another ghost, who insisted on shaking hands. He had a glove stuffed with wet sand on a stick, and you got that "creepy" feeling when you grasped the clammy thing.

A witch waited at the door downstairs. She was introduced to each one and mumbled the name over to herself.

A committee at the door attended to the introducing and then wrote the names of the arrivals on slips of paper, pinning these on the proper ones.

1. As this was a crowd where a good many were unacquainted, a *get-acquainted stunt* was in order. The girls formed an outer circle, the boys an inner circle, and marched in opposite directions to piano music. When the piano stopped, as it did at frequent intervals, the marchers stopped, faced one another, each learned the other's name, and they conversed until the piano began playing, when they resumed the march.

2. A ring, thimble, and penny had been hidden about the room, and the players were told to hunt them. When found they were informed that finding the ring indicated early marriage, the thimble single blessedness, and the penny wealth.

3. *Fête of Famous Ghosts.*—The witch called certain folks to meet with the Witches' Council. The Witches' Council, composed of the witches and a few members of the Social Committee, explained to the group chosen just what each was to do. The idea was to represent famous characters by covering the head with an old pillow casing in which eyes had been cut, and the body with a sheet, and indicating some telltale characteristic in some way. The persons called out by the witch impersonated these ghosts.

The rest of the crowd were provided with paper and pencil and guessed the names of the famous ghosts.

(1) George Washington, who walked across the platform carrying a hatchet and a bunch of cherries.

(2) Eve, carrying an apple and dragging a toy snake across the floor.

(3) Queen Elizabeth and Sir Walter Raleigh. Sir Walter put down a cloak (white rag), upon which the Queen crossed an imaginary mud puddle.

(4) Diogenes, carrying a lantern.

(5) Darwin, looking for the missing link.

(6) Betsy Ross, sewing on American flag.

(7) Napoleon, with white hat (paper) and folded arms.

(8) Benjamin Franklin, with kite and key.

(9) Theodore Roosevelt, with a big stick.

(10) Carrie Nation. The witch stepped out and put up a sign with "Saloon" printed on it. Ghost carried rubber hatchet (obtainable at most ten-cent stores), destroyed the furniture in pantomime, and completed her wrecking expedition by knocking down the sign and trampling on it.

4. A short, creepy ghost story was told by the witch, the crowd seated about on the floor, no light being furnished except such as came from a pan of salt saturated with alcohol.

5. *Blowing Out Candle.*—Blindfold boy and girl. Turn them about and let them endeavor to blow out a lighted candle.

6. Fortune-telling stunts:

(1) Pumpkin with letters of the alphabet cut in it. Hang it from the transom of a door. Spin and let each take turn sticking a hatpin in it. The letter stabbed indicates the initial of the future life partner.

(2) Three dishes are placed on a table, one with clear water, one with soapy water, the third empty. Blindfold participants. Lead them to the table and allow each one to touch a dish. If the finger is put in the clear water, it foretells happy marriage; soapy, marry a widow or widower; empty, single cussedness.

(3) Write fortunes on paper with lemon juice, which makes excellent invisible ink. One at a time each person visits the witch, who mumbles a few unintelligible words, then passes one of the strips of paper over a lighted candle and hands to the person waiting. Lo, the words of a fortune have appeared on what seemed to be a blank piece of paper!

Refreshments.—Apples, ginger snaps, and "witch's brew" (lemonade with a little grape juice or loganberry juice added).

HALLOWE'EN FROLIC

Decorations.—Remember that Hallowe'en decorations are necessary to the proper Hallowe'en atmosphere.

Bobbing for Apples.—In order to break up that awkward period when you are waiting for the crowd to gather, start guests to bobbing for apples floating in a big tub of water. On each apple is cut or pinned an initial.

Chamber of Horrors.—Next the guests are conducted two at a time through the Chamber of Horrors, a dark room or passageway where all sorts of creepy things happen. There is a rattling of chains, a terrifying noise made by scraping pieces of tin together, a ghost-guide who has a tantalizing way of frightening you with the use of a feather duster, though, of course, you don't know it's a feather duster. Then there is a giant ghost whose very presence is "scary" and everything. He may be standing on stilts with back against the wall, and occasionally he moans piteously. Off in one dark corner every now and then two eyes flame for a second. These have been made by using empty eggshells in which have been inserted tiny electric light bulbs, which are flashed on and off. The ghost-guide tells a pitiful story about a friend who has died and makes each one handle parts of the dead man's body. These parts are kept on plates placed on a long table or on chairs. The guide may direct the victim's hands to each plate. It will not be necessary to lift the parts. As he comes to each one he moans and sobs out that "these are his poor dear eyes," etc. If you don't think this is some creepy experience, try it. The eyes are two hulled grapes, the tongue a raw oyster, the heart a piece of liver, the lungs a wet sponge, the brain a coil of rope dampened or a part of an ear of green corn.

Pumpkin Head Game.—Make a pumpkin head out of heavy cardboard. Make a large cut-out mouth. Tack a wooden frame to your pumpkin head and a standard, so that it will stand in an erect or slanting position as desired. The crowd should be divided into two sides, and each player attempts to toss, by an underhand throw, a tennis ball through the pumpkin's mouth.

Spook Show.—A clever spook show could be worked out. Two spooks capture a person who, on being asked his name, answers "Sam," and on a further demand for his other name tremblingly informs his captors that his "maiden name is Johnson." Mephisto and a ghost chorus now enter the scene of action, and one of the ghosts informs the captive that he need not fear, for it's no one but "Mephistopheles." "Mephiswhoforlee?" queries Sam. "Mephisto, Mephistopheles." "Well," answers Sam, "it looks like the devil to me." The ghost chorus may then sing slowly and as spookily as possible to the tune of "Auld Lang Syne":

"We're looking for young men, young men
Who plan to take no wife.
We'll put them in a dungeon dark
And keep them there for life.

We're looking for young folks, young folks
Who mutter and complain.
We'll put them at hard work and toil;
They'll have real aches and pains."

Sam, during the singing of this song, may protest his innocence of the crimes mentioned.

A number of local "hits" may be pulled off by having the two chief ghosts act as questioners and Sam as the "gag" man.

As a special feature of the show someone may recite or sing "Little Orphant Annie" by James Whitcomb Riley. ("An' the Gobble-uns'll git you ef you don't watch out!")

A spook male quartet can be formed from members of the group. By practicing beforehand, they can sing one or two Hallowe'en songs very effectively. Solo selections may also be used.

Jumping the Candles.—A dozen lighted candles are placed about two feet apart in a row across the room. Each candle represents a month. The young ladies are to hop from side to side over these, the candle that is snuffed out indicating the month of marriage. This feature should precede the spook show, that being the closing feature of your program. Serve wieners and rye bread or ginger snaps and sweet cider.

OTHER HALLOWE'EN SUGGESTIONS

One organization had three fortune-telling booths. In one was a fortune wheel. This may be made by pinning an indicator on a piece of cardboard which has been marked off in twelve sections. The number at which the indicator points when it stops spinning indicates some fortune, a list being posted where all can read it. In another booth was a witch with the invisible ink fortunes which she "hocus-pocused" over a lighted candle. In still another booth was a gypsy palmist, who happened to be one of the members, who got off clever things because she knew a little about palmistry and a lot about her crowd.

Apple Seeds

Name two wet apple seeds and stick them on the fore head. The first seed to fall off indicates that the person for whom it is named is not true.

Apple Seed Jingle

The number of seeds in the apple tell the fortune after this fashion:

> "One, I love; two, I love;
> Three, I love, I say;
> Four, I love with all my heart;
> Five, I cast away;
> Six, he loves; seven, she loves;
> Eight, they both agree;
> Nine, he comes; ten, he tarries;
> Eleven, he courts; twelve, he marries."

Fortune-Telling Peanuts

Prepare these by removing the nuts and putting in tiny folded bits of paper on which are written such words as "journey," "wealth," "success," "brunette," "blonde," etc. Give one to each guest.

Yarn Test

Each girl drops a ball of yarn (ordinary string or thread will answer in a pinch) over the banister or balcony, holding tightly to one end and remaining unseen. The boys scramble for the ball, and when the yarn is drawn taut the girl calls: "Who holds?" The boy must reply with his true name. If the girl drops the end she holds, she will remain unmarried. If the yarn breaks, she will not marry any of those present. This scheme may also be used to arrange partners for refreshments.

Counting Seeds

Each one is given an apple. The apple is to be cut in two, crossways, and the seeds counted. If two seeds are found, it indicates early marriage; three legacy; four, greath wealth; five, ocean trip; six, great public fame; seven, possession of any gift most desired by finder.

Bean Fortune

Give out little sacks of beans, making no effort to count them. Each person may tell his or her own fortune then after the manner in which we used to count off buttons on our coats:

'Rich man, poor man, beggar man, thief,
Doctor, lawyer, merchant, chief.

Rich girl, poor girl, beggar girl, crook,
Schoolgirl, 'phone girl, servant girl, cook.

This year, next year, no year, darn;
Big house, little house, hotel, barn.''

A Giant Ghost

At one party a giant ghost met every one as he stepped into the room. He was tremendously tall and looked very funny when he bowed almost to the floor. He also had a peculiar habit of dwindling in size until he appeared only of normal height. Here is the secret: A ghost's head had been fastened on the end of a broom, a sheet was fastened about it at the neck, and the entire thing held up by a girl or boy inside, who held the broom by the handle, raising or lowering it at pleasure.

A Goblin Party

Why not have a goblin party and have the guests come wearing a covering of sheets and old pillow slips? Number the goblins as they arrive, pinning the number on the breast. Pass out paper and pencils and let each one make his guess as to who's who, putting down the number and name. When sufficient time has been allowed for this, have each one in turn, beginning with number one, step before the crowd and unmask. Each player will check up on his own paper. The one making the most correct list may be awarded some prize.

A BLACK-CAT PARTY

Invitation.—"The black cats are going to convene Monday evening, October 31, at eight o'clock. Be on hand for the fun." (Name of organization, date and place.)

Decorate with all sorts and sizes of paper black cats. Play "Poor Little Pussy Cat," "Pussy Wants a Corner," "Cat and Mouse," and "The Minister's Cat." The latter game is played after this fashion: The players seat themselves about in a circle, with one player in the center. He throws a knotted handkerchief at one of the players and says: "The minister's cat is——." The player hit must finish the sentence with some word descriptive of the cat and beginning with the letter "A." Thus he answers: "An ambitious cat," "An agile cat," "An ancient cat," etc. Failure to respond at once or repetition of an adjective already used puts one out of the game. This is kept up until only one player is able to respond. When one letter is exhausted another may be chosen.

The following "cat" contest may be used:

1. A cat in a deluge? Cataclysm.
2. A cat in a place of burial? Catacomb.
3. A Roman cat? Cataline.
4. A cat that has fits? Cataleptic.
5. A tree cat? Catalpa.
6. A library cat? Catalogue.
7. A climbing cat? Catamount.

8. A water cat? Cataract.
9. A cat that needs to be doctored? Catarrh.
10. A cat in trouble? Catastrophe.
11. A cat in pleasing popular melody? Catchy.
12. A religious cat? Catechism.
13. A classified cat? Category.
14. A cat in fruit stores? Catawba.
15. A table cat? Catsup.

The Black-Cat Society may now be organized, the first thing in order being the election of a Chief Howler. Make the election as exciting and amusing as possible by the nomination of several people, having some one present the claims of each. The Chief Howler now takes charge and commands all brother and sister black cats to join in the society anthem. He then begins:

> 'Three blind mice,
> Three blind mice.
> See how they run,
> See how they run.
> They all ran after the farmer's wife,
> She cut off their tails with a carving knife.
> Three blind mice,'' etc.

The person to the right of the Chief Howler begins the song for himself by the time the Chief Howler has reached the second line. And so with the person to the right of this one, and all the way around, each singing with complacent disregard of the other. Over and over they sing it. It ought to be a "howling success." The Chief Howler raps for order when he figures the society anthem has been given its due emphasis and announces: "All in favor of adjourning for 'eats' say 'Meow.'" All the black cats answer with a chorus of "Meows," of course.

Sweet milk and pie may be served. A milk-drinking contest may be put on, with some of the boys as contestants.

The milk should be poured into saucers, and the contestants must "lap" it up like a cat.

MEETING THE QUEEN OF HALLOWE'EN

All guests, one at a time, must appear before the Queen of Hallowe'en, kneel, and lift the right hand for her blessing. The queen, with pasteboard crown, sits on her throne over in one corner. She wears on her right hand a glove, which has sewed in its palm a copper wire, off the end of which has been scraped the insulation. This wire runs around back of her to the floor, where it is connected with a battery. This battery is so arranged that the queen can throw on the "juice" by stepping on a switch. The switch and battery, of course, are covered by her dress. As the victim kneels and extends his hand, the queen grasps it as if to shake hands, throws on the switch, and the subject leaps to his feet with a wild yell.

CHAPTER XI

NOVEMBER PROGRAMS

A FOOTBALL SOCIAL

Each one as he comes in has a number pinned on his back, football style. Two sets of numbers have been provided—namely, A and B sets. Girls get even numbers, boys odd. Thus 1-A or 1-B would be a boy, and 2-A or 2-B would be a girl.

1. *Get Acquainted.*—Form two circles, girls inner, boys outer. March to music in opposite directions. When the music stops, marchers stop and face each other. Each shouts his or her own name in a loud voice. They converse until the music starts. Then as it starts each one shouts the name of the person opposite and begins to march as before.

2. *Football Guessing Contest.*—Answers are to be made in musical terms:

(1) What does the line need to do when hard pressed? Brace.

(2) What decides the game? Score.

(3) What kind of a football player does the coach call a man who on his first time out plays a fine game? Natural.

(4) What does a football player who has been punched in the stomach need? Air.

(5) With the score a tie, for what does the better team pray? Time.

(6) What does each team want to do? Beat.

(7) What do players do on a muddy field when tackled? Slide.

(8) What do players do between quarters? Rest.

(9) What is the coaching squad sometimes called? Staff.

(10) What is a game where neither side scores? Tie.

(11) What do they often do to determine whether or not a team has made first down? Measure.

(12) Of what two terms would you be reminded by a back field dressed in polka dot jerseys? Dotted quarter and dotted half.

(13) What kind of head often spoils a good player? Swell.

(14) For whom does she root at the game? Hymn (him).

3. *Shouting Proverbs.*—Call out several groups of six numbers each, calling three odd and three even numbers for each group. These groups then decide, each, on some proverb of six words, as, for instance: "Make hay while the sun shines," "All that glitters is not gold," "A stitch in time saves nine." Each person in the group is given one word of the proverb, and by one group at a time the proverb is shouted, each person in the group shouting his word simultaneously with the others in the group. The rest of the crowd guesses what the proverb is.

4. *Surprise Quartets.*—Call for groups of four members each, calling two odd and two even numbers for each group. These groups form quartets and must sing some song of their own selection. After each of the four quartets has performed, all four sing at the same time, each singing its own song. The judges, previously appointed, decide which is the worst quartet and give it some adequate recognition.

5. *Championship Football Contest between the A's and B's.*—Cover table with green paper or cloth. Mark off like a football field, placing goal posts at each end. These can be easily made out of sticks of wood. Empty an eggshell of its contents and color it brown. Mark seams and lacing with ink so as to make the shell resemble a football as much as possible. It might be well to have another in reserve, so no interruption of the game will be occasioned by the breaking of the shell. The shell is placed in the center of the field, and contestants take turn in trying to blow it through the goal posts at the opponent's end of the table. Each successful attempt scores a touchdown for the team making it. The ball is placed in mid-field each time.

Each side should select eleven players to represent them. The first half shall be considered played when each contestant on the two elevens has blown once. The game is ended when each team has had two chances for each member of the team.

A variation of this plan is to place the ball in mid-field and at the sound of the whistle to have all the members of each team begin to blow. In this case a touchdown is scored when the ball goes over the goal line in bounds. When the ball is blown out of bounds, the referee puts it back out from the point where it went out of bounds. When the ball goes out of bounds, neither team is to begin to blow until the referee's whistle shall sound. Breaking this rule shall be considered an off-side play, and a penalty of "five yards" will be made.

The two sides are expected to root for their representatives during the progress of the game.

ANOTHER FOOTBALL GAME

1. Mark out on the floor a football field with "ten-yard lines."

2. *Equipment.*—A football, a baseball, and twenty-two Indian clubs or long-necked bottles; two sets of eleven slips of paper each, on which the following plays are written:

(1) Forward pass, ten yards.
(2) Penalty for holding, ten yards.
(3) End run, thirty yards.
(4) Penalty for off-side play, five yards.
(5) Line plunges, fifteen yards.
(6) Penalty for slugging, fifteen yards.
(7) Penalty for coaching from the side lines, ten yards.
(8) "Safety," score two.
(9) Touchdown, score six.
(10) Field goal, score three.
(11) Penalty for unnecessary roughness to player receiving a forward pass, ten yards.

3. The company is divided into two groups. Eleven players represent each group. A yell leader should be appointed for each side and should keep enthusiasm at a high pitch.

4. At each goal line eleven Indian clubs are placed in a row a foot apart, and one of the prepared written plays is placed under each club.

5. The players line up behind the clubs.

6. Captains draw for first play.

7. The football is placed in the middle of the "field," and the baseball is given to the captain of the side to play first. That captain rolls the ball at the opponents' Indian clubs. Three trials may be allowed. If the ball knocks down or hits a club, the slip beneath indicates the play. The umpire moves the football accordingly, registering

either a penalty or a gain. Each player tries in turn, the sides alternating in rolling the ball.

8. A scorekeeper keeps account of the scores made.

9. One time around may be considered a quarter. At the end of the half the ball goes back to the center, before the third quarter begins.

HARVEST HOME SOCIAL

Have the guests come dressed in country costumes of sundry character. For instance, there may be the village gossip, the village conscience, the village belle, the village old maid, the country dude, the farmer, storekeeper, constable, etc. Award a prize for the best make-up. Lanterns, oil lamps, and candles are used for lights. Stalks of corn, pumpkins, ears of corn, and autumn leaves serve as decorations. Play rollicking old-fashioned games, such as "The Jolly Miller," "Drop the Handkerchief," "Jacob and Rachel," "Going to Jerusalem," etc. A pumpkin seed hunt may be used to begin the fun.

The *Village Orchestra* may perform at some place in the evening's program. Each one chooses an imaginary instrument. The leader announces the tune and then begins playing, making appropriate noise and movement for the instrument he selects. All players play their respective instruments in the same manner. The leader may be playing the flute. If he stops suddenly and begins playing the violin, then the violin player must take up the flute. The leader may change any time the notion strikes him. Any player failing to make the changes at the proper time must pay a forfeit.

A *Village Scandal* may be enacted by having a mock trial in which Mr. Cy Sweeter may be tried for breach of promise. Miss Sadie Soothum is the plaintiff, and Judge Heeza Pest presides. The notables of the village are called in as witnesses. Squire Skinner acts as prosecutor and Hon. Hezekiah Goose as attorney for the defendant.

Serve sandwiches, cookies, and coffee.

A THANKSGIVING PARTY

Decorate with chrysanthemums, corn, pumpkins, autumn leaves, footballs, fruit, vegetables, etc. Each one may be asked to bring some donation in food or clothing to be used by the Social Service Committee in helping the needy.

As each guest arrives have him write on a slip of paper his name and a number which indicates his guess on the number of petals on a large chrysanthemum in a vase near by. The paper is then pinned on the guesser and serves as an "ice breaker." After the apple race the petals may be counted and the winner awarded a chrysanthemum or some other inexpensive prize.

The Apple Race is next in order. Divide your party into two or more sides. Have them stand in straight lines facing one another and some four feet apart. An apple is given the leader of each line. At a given signal each starts the apple down his line, placing it with two hands into the two hands of the person next to him. This person passes it to the next in the same manner, and so on down the line. The end person receives it and then runs as fast as possible to the head of the line, starting the apple down once more. This is continued until one side has had all of its players run with the apple, thus getting the original No. 1 back at the head. Players run on the inside of the lines.

Now count your chrysanthemum petals before the crowd and announce the winner of the guessing contest.

Pass paper and pencils and give every one ten minutes to see how many words can be made out of the letters in "chrysanthemum." Fix up a pasteboard imitation medal with the inscription, "Champion Word Slinger, November ——, 1920, —— [place, State]," and pin this on the breast of the winner.

Now announce that you have a mysterious bottle that never fails to answer questions correctly. The entire group forms a circle. One person stands in the center with a bottle, which is one of the long-necked kind. A large grape juice bottle will be just the thing. A Coca-Cola bottle will do. The person in the center asks the bottle a question, such as "Who is most deeply in love in this crowd?" or "Who has received the most proposals?" or "Who has the biggest ears?" He then spins the bottle on its side. The one to whom it points when it stops indicates its answer. This person now exchanges places with the person in the center, and the game continues as long as desired.

Now try pinning the head on a turkey. Have a large picture of the Thanksgiving bird, minus the head, pinned on a sheet or curtain. Give each one a chance to pin the head in proper place after being blindfolded.

Feather Football.—Now let the players divide into two sides and gather at opposite ends of a large table. In the center of the table is a downy feather. Players on both sides blow against one another in trying to get the feather over the opponent's goal. They may creep up as far as the middle of the table, but no farther. Should the feather go out of bounds—that is, off one side or the other—it is put in play out from the point where it went outside.

Serve fruit salad and wafers.

"PASS IT"

Play "Pass It," using November articles.

A PILGRIM PARTY

Make this a costume party and have the guests come dressed in Pilgrim fashion or as American Indians. You might have Priscilla and John Alden receive folks at the door.

Pilgrim Scramble

When the guests have arrived pass out sets of letters to each one, seven letters in a set. The letters in each set will all be the same. Thus there will be seven P's in a set, or seven I's, etc. One letter, known only to the chairman or to the committee, will be your key letter. For instance, you select "G" as your key letter. Then you would have only one set of this letter. Of the others you would have as many sets as are required to supply your crowd, there being several of each, at least. As soon as all the sets are distributed a general scramble ensues, in which the players exchange letters with a view to getting the letters which will spell "Pilgrim." As soon as a player has the necessary letters he reports to the chairman. It will be possible for only seven players to accomplish this, since only seven G's are available. Each of the seven lucky ones may be awarded some sort of prize, such as a chrysanthemum, toy turkey, and the like.

Thanksgiving Menu

Pass out papers and pencils and let the players work on the following menu:

1. *Soup.*—Imitation reptile, or what the slangy boy carries on his shoulders for a head.

2. *Fish.*—"Collect on delivery," or a good thing from which to come down.

3. *Roasts.*—The country of the Crescent and Adam's wife, served with a sauce of what undid her.

4. *Vegetables.*—Two kinds of toes ne'er found on man or beast; a mild term for stealing; what your heart does, popular in Boston.

5. *Pudding.*—What we say to a nuisance, and much sought by political job hunters.

6. *Pies.*—An affected gait, and related to a well.

7. *Fruit.*—A kind of shot.

8. *Drink.*—A sign of a cold and what the minister expects when he performs a wedding ceremony.

Answers

1. Mock turtle, bean.
2. Cod, perch.
3. Turkey, spare rib with apple sauce.
4. Potatoes, tomatoes, cabbage, beats, beans.
5. Sago, plum.
6. Mince, pumpkin.
7. Grape.
8. Coffee.

Pilgrim Pictures

Make a huge frame. Stand this out from the wall some distance, say ten feet, with long sticks running back on either side from the top of the frame to the wall, thus holding the frame in place. These sticks also serve as a framework for the top and side covering. Cover the front of the frame with mosquito netting and the sides and top with dark blankets. Arrange a light in this inclosure so that it will shine on the poser. Have the frame curtained, letting pages in costume pull the curtain aside when the picture is ready. All light should be turned off except the light in the inclosure. If the instructions are followed as outlined, the tableaux will be very effective.

The following pictures and songs may be given:

1. *The Pilgrim.*—Have some one sing one verse of "Faith

of Our Fathers" as a solo during the showing of this picture. The one taking the part of Pilgrim should carry a Bible under one arm and a gun under the other.

2. *The First American.*—Some one in Indian costume who stands peering into the distance, one hand shading his eyes.

Song.—Have some one sing as a solo "By the Waters of Minnetonka," by Lieurance, or "The Land of the Sky-Blue Water," by Cadman.

3. *Priscilla.*—A girl in old-fashioned Pilgrim garb poses as some one sings "Ah, Believe Me if All Those Endearing Young Charms."

4. *The Attack.*—In this picture the girl appears kneeling in petition before the Indian, who stands with dagger or tomahawk in hand in threatening attitude.

5. *The Rescue.*—Indian, Girl, Pilgrim. The Indian lies prostrate in death; the girl stands with arms outstretched to her deliverer, who stands with gun in hand.

6. *The End of a Perfect Day.*—Girl and Pilgrim pose facing one another and holding hands. Girl looks down and Pilgrim is looking intently into her face. Have quartet sing "A Perfect Day," by Carrie Jacobs-Bond.

Brewster's Message

Now have some one read Elder Brewster's message to the Pilgrims when he bade them be true to their promises: "Blessed will it be for us, blessed for this land, for this vast continent. Nay, from generation to generation will the blessings descend. Generations to come will look back to this hour and these scenes of agonizing trial, to this day of small things, and say: 'Here was our beginning as a people. These were our forefathers. Through their trials we inherit our blessings. Their faith is our faith, their hope our hope, their God our God.' "

Refreshments

Pumpkin pie and sweet milk.

Some Forfeits

1. Keep on yawning until you can make somebody else yawn.
2. Call your sweetheart's name up the chimney.
3. Say the alphabet backwards.
4. Stand in the middle of the room in any position six people put you in.
5. Say "She sells seashells on the seashore" three times without making a mistake.
6. Stand on a chair and make a speech on any subject the hostess proposes.
7. Tell each person in the room what you in turn think of him or her.

CHAPTER XII

DECEMBER PROGRAMS

Snow Frolic
Christmas Snowballs
Some Suggestions for that Christmas Party

SNOW FROLIC

Social for December

Decorations.—Cover the floor with white, using old sheets, cheesecloth, or a borrowed tarpaulin. Sprinkle the floor with tinsel. Festoon the room with white. Make a snow man by covering two bushel baskets with white. Make head by stuffing an old pillowcase, marking with ink eyes, nose, and mouth, and placing an old pipe in the mouth. Make this snow man as realistic as possible and place him in a conspicuous position. Stuff inexpensive presents in around his neck, tying them to white and red strings that shall hang outside. The white strings shall be for the girls, the red for the boys. After the ice-guessing contest have each girl and each boy visit the snow man to get a present.

The first feature of the evening's fun will be an "Icicle Game." Have a wire stretched across the room. Tie sticks of candy on it. Blindfold the young people as they arrive, hand each a pair of scissors, and let them attempt to clip an "icicle." Participants are not allowed to feel around for the wire, but must clip wherever they stop.

Divide the crowd into two sides for the snowball-throwing. This can be done rapidly by having them draw from a hat slips on which are written either "White" or "Gold." Captains are appointed for the two teams, and they line up for the contest. A target is provided by tacking a sheet on the wall. In the center is a black piece of cheesecloth about one foot in diameter. Contestants stand at a distance of something like fifteen feet and toss a tennis ball, which has been dipped in a plate of flour, at the target. Every hit in the black center counts a point, the sides taking turn in throwing.

Announce now that you are to have a snowstorm. In the beginning of the evening you have given to each girl a small circular piece of white paper on which was written a number. This, you told her, was her "snowflake," and that she would need it later in the evening. You didn't explain further. Following your announcement of the "snowstorm," some one goes to the balcony or stands on a chair and calls all the young men to gather beneath him. He has a handful of "snowflakes," duplicates of the ones given out to the girls. Each man is instructed to get a snowflake as they descend. He then searches for the girl with the duplicate number, and she becomes his "snowflake" for the rest of the evening's fun.

Each young man and his "snowflake" now work together on an ice-guessing contest. It is represented in words that end in "ice" or "ise":

1. The ice of inducement. Entice.
2. The fussy ice. Precise.
3. The ice most feared by womankind. Mice.
4. The ice of games. Dice.
5. The ice that should satisfy. Suffice.
6. The ice of religious worship. Sacrifice.
7. The aromatic ice. Spice.
8. The ice of established value. Price.
9. The ice of invention. Device.

10. The ice among grain. Rice.
11. The miser's ice. Avarice.
12. The ice of habit. Practice.
13. The ice of the faithful Epworth Leaguer. Service.
14. Heavenly ice. Paradise.
15. The ice of peacemakers. Armistice.

Immediately on the completion of this contest announce that the next event will be a "Frost." Invite about six couples to go out of the room. Explain to the rest of the crowd the nature of the "frost" and then call in one of the persons sent out of the room. A chair has been arranged. A boy is brought in and directed to the chair, behind which stands a pretty girl. He is then blindfolded. A young man, previously selected, steps noiselessly over from the crowd and kisses the blindfolded victim lightly on the cheek, dropping immediately back into the crowd. The blindfold is taken off, and the young man looks around to see the pretty girl still standing behind the chair. He is invited to take his place with the crowd. A young lady is brought in. A young man stands behind the chair, and a young lady steps over from the crowd and perpetrates the "frost." Screams of laughter greet this performance.

Refreshments.—Ice cream and frosted cake. Pop corn balls may also be used.

It would be lots of fun to give this social in the spring or summer for the novelty of the thing. In that case thermometers imbedded in ice should be placed in conspicuous positions, and the strings about the snow man's neck, instead of having presents, would have fortunes tied to them.

CHRISTMAS SNOWBALLS

Divide your crowd into two sides. Line the players up and give a basket decorated with holly and ribbon to the leader of each group. Place on the floor before each line a row of five cotton snowballs. The race is now to be run after the fashion of a potato race. The first person picks up the snowballs, puts them in the basket, and returns to deliver the basket to the next in line. This person now replaces the snowballs on the floor in proper place. And so on it goes until every player has run the course.

SOME SUGGESTIONS FOR THAT CHRISTMAS PARTY

Christmas Decorations.—Tastefully decorate with holly, mistletoe, and red and green crêpe paper. Of course you will want a Christmas tree to give the finished effect.

Christmas Presents.—Write the names of all the members of the Club on slips of paper. A week or so before the party have each one draw a name. Boys' and girls' names may be kept separate if you desire. The drawer is supposed to bring a present to the party for the person whose name appears on his slip. No present shall cost more than ten cents. The giver may exercise his ingenuity in wrapping the present as well as in addressing it. The packages are all turned in on arrival and later in the evening Santa Claus distributes them. All packages must be opened in full view of the crowd. A few extra packages should be on hand for persons who may not be members of the Club and whose names therefore may not have been handed in. The opening of the packages should occasion a bit of merriment.

Christmas Bells.—Give each guest on arrival ten tiny

red paper bells. During the evening any time he can get some one to answer him with a "Yes" or "No" he collects a bell from them, and any time he is forgetful and is tricked into answering "Yes" or "No" he must surrender a bell to the person who has caught him. At the close of the time allotted for this game some prize is awarded to the person having the largest number of bells in his possession. A variation of this plan is to allow this feature to extend through the entire evening.

Christmas Pantomimes.—Divide your crowd into three groups, the Jingles, the Bells, and the Santas. This may be done by having them line up and count off by threes, thus: "One, two, three; one, two, three." All the ones would form one group, all the twos another, and all the threes the third group. Instruct each group now to plan some sort of original Christmas pantomime. Any activity or presentation representative of the Christmas season will answer. Judges will decide which group presents the best pantomime.

Snowball Fight.—Each of the three groups now select ten players to represent them in the Snowball Fight. The players sit by teams, nine in each row. The extra player assumes a position about ten feet in front of his team and midway between the end players. These players are each supplied with a large cotton ball. At the signal to start the players seated at the left end of each line stand erect and the pivot players toss the cotton balls to them. Catching the ball the end man rushes to the pivot position with it. The former pivot man in the meantime has rushed for the opposite end of the line and has seated himself, all the players having slid up one. The new pivot man turns as soon as he reaches the pivot position and tosses to the man who has slid into his position. The ball must always be received in an upright position so each player as he reaches the chair on the left end immediately arises to receive the toss. The first team to have the original pivot man back at that position is winner

Santa's Toy Shop.—Assemble all the girls in one room and all the boys in another. Whisper to each girl the name of some toy. Have some one else at the same time give the names of the same list of toys to the boys. When the girls are admitted to the toy-shop each boy represents the toy given him by some appropriate action or sound. Each girl walks about the shop seeking to find the particular toy awarded her, taking charge of it as soon as it is located. Thus each lady and her "toy" become partners for refreshments.

CHAPTER XIII

SPECIAL SUMMER PROGRAM SUGGESTIONS

If I were Recreational Leader for the Summer:

1. I would take my job seriously.

2. I would study and make research in the best books on socials and games in order to know what to do.

3. I would ask that a live committee be appointed to help me.

4. I would determine that no affair given under our auspices would be a failure for lack of thorough planning.

5. I would call my committee together and plan for the liveliest summer of fun that is possible.

6. I would promote class and group affairs.

7. I would cooperate with others in the church and community in order to avoid hurtful competition and overlapping.

8. At the committee meeting I would put in the hands of each member of the committee an outline of possibilities that would start their tongues to wagging, discussing the things we should do.

9. I would advertise our good times with posters, special invitations, and snappy announcements. What's the use of all our planning if the young people don't come?

10. I would pray over my work, for by it I would hope to build into our young people Christian attitudes—loyalty, enthusiasm, friendliness, cooperation, cheerfulness, and fellowship with the Master.

These would be my ten guide-posts. I would keep them constantly before myself and my committee.

Now I am ready to talk about definite plans. I find a world of possibilities, and so I would jot them down for my convenience and the convenience of the committee. These are:

1. Parties—Lawn, porch, pavilion, barn.
2. Picnics—Moonlight, afternoon, all-day.
3. Excursions—Launch parties, river excursions, railroad to some point of interest, fishing trips, etc.
4. Summer Camps—Many churches are now promoting camps of a week or ten days for their young people.
5. Athletics—Baseball teams, volleyball, tennis tournaments, field meets, swimming.
6. Playground Activities—Some of the above. Also croquet, clock-golf, pig-in-the-hole, horseshoe or quoits tournament.
7. Community singing, along with high-class instrumental and vocal selections by the best artists obtainable.
8. Open-air Dramatics—Pageants, short plays, tableaux, pantomimes.
9. Hikes and hay-rides.
10. Camp-fires.

With this list before me I am ready now to outline my suggestions of possibilities for each month.

June
- Flower Lawn Party.
- Moonlight Picnic.
- Field Meet.
- Book Costume Party.

July
- Community Sing.
- Open-air Dramatic Evening.
- Fourth of July Picnic.
- Trip Around the World.

August:
- Watermelon Festival.
- Hay-ride.
- Tennis Tournament
- Camera Hike.
- Indian Party and Camp Fire.
- Quoits or Horse-shoe Tournament.

Our committee, after some live discussion, decides what features it will promote during the summer. Croquet, volley-ball, base-ball, tennis, and horse-shoes are chosen as activities that are to run through the entire season. A baseball team is to be organized by the boys to play each week. A vacant lot near the church is to be cleaned up and fitted for a playground. Here tennis, volley-ball, croquet, horse-shoe pitching, and playground ball are to be played.

Our next job now is to lay definite plans for the month of June. The Flower Lawn Social is discussed and outlined. Or it may be that some of the other suggestions for that month are chosen.

FLOWER LAWN SOCIAL

Decorations.—Japanese lanterns. Plenty of flowers and plants.

1. *Here We Go Round the Mulberry Bush.*—All join hands, forming large circle around the lawn, and skipping to the left as they sing to the tune of "Here We Go Round the Mulberry Bush":

(1) Here we go round the mulberry bush, the mulberry bush, the mulberry bush;
Here we go round the mulberry bush, so early in the evening.

(2) (Skipping to the right.)
This is the way we clap our hands, we clap our hands, we clap our hands;

This is the way we clap our hands, so early in the evening.

(Piano should repeat music as all clap in time.)

(3) (All bow first to partners, and then to persons on other side of them as they sing):

This is the way we greet our friends, we greet our friends, we greet our friends;
This is the way we greet our friends, so early in the evening.

(4) Skip, repeating verse number one.

2. *Flower Charades.*—Divide the crowd into several groups and have each group present two or three flower charades while the others guess. When the flower is correctly guessed the performing group is chased back to a given line called the garden wall. All players captured become members of the capturing team. Flowers that may be used are rose, aster, primrose, Johnny-jump-up, poppy, goldenrod, chrysanthemum, marigold, trumpet, balsam, elder, sweet William, bachelor's button, tulips, forget-me-not, lady's slipper, sweet peas, and wandering Jew.

3. *Sunflower Song Show.*—The participants will, of course, be fitted out with stiff, wide, yellow petal collars giving the sunflower effect. If yellow cardboard is not available, cover the petals with yellow paper or cloth. Or all participants may stick their heads through an opening in a long strip of cloth. Around each opening has been fashioned a large sunflower, by sewing yellow petals on the cloth. When the curtain is drawn aside all the sunflowers may be feigning sleep. Slowly they open their eyes, then roll eyes right, then left, then up, then front. The opening number should now be sung. "Where the Morning Glories Grow" would make a good number. Other good song numbers would be "My Wild Irish Rose," "Love

Brings a Little Gift of Roses," "Remember the Rose," "The Last Rose of Summer," etc. Some good jokes, with a local flavor, if possible, would intersperse the song numbers.

4. *Refreshments.*—Ice cream with rose or other flower standing in it. Cakes with icing flowers.

Fourth of July Picnic

Get the whole church to come together for a gala day packed with fun and good fellowship. The church will be all the better for this one big play day all together.

Games that can be played are Dodge Ball (Bancroft, 364), "Three Deep," "Jacob and Rachel," "Three Legged Race," "Spanish Relay," "Blind Swat," "Rooster Fight." See also other relay races and games in Phunology. Remember it is important to plan your program definitely.

There ought to be a short patriotic speech and a flag-raising exercise. At the flag-raising some good reader could give "Your Flag and My Flag," or Riley's "Old Glory."

It would be a good idea also to send up several tissue-paper balloons toward dusk.

Community Singing

During the war community singing became a popular and effective means for stirring the fires of patriotism, at the same time affording a delightful diversion and a helpful relaxation from the strain of war conditions. In "Y" huts, in parks, in public buildings, everywhere, soldiers and civilians were gathered together to sing. The slogan was "A singing army and a singing people can't be defeated."

Community singing has tremendous value also as a peace-time recreation. Perhaps you could get together all the churches in your community for an out-door sing once a month during the summer.

A good song leader would be necessary to insure success, and a good pianist also is essential.

Song sheets could be printed or they may be obtained at nominal cost from Community Service, 315 Fourth Avenue, New York City. Some fine suggestions are contained in a booklet entitled "Community Singing," issued by that organization.

Remember that the most popular songs are the old songs. The truth of this statement was attested in a recent vote that was taken in various parts of the country by community song directors. In the list of eighteen highest were "Dixie," "Old Folks at Home," "America, The Beautiful," "Old Kentucky Home," "Carry Me Back to Old Virginny," "Old Black Joe," "Sweet Genevieve," and other songs. "There's a Long, Long Trail," "L'il Liza Jane," "Sweet Adeline," "Good-night Ladies," and " 'Till We Meet Again" were also in this list of eighteen.

A singing contest might be arranged between several of the churches as a special feature for one evening.

Another special feature that may be added to your program is to have a pantomime of some such song as "Rock of Ages," or "Abide With Me," while a quartet sings the song.

Some good special musical numbers should feature every program.

Open Air Bible Dramatic Evening

This would arouse a great deal of interest and would afford an evening both pleasant and profitable. It might be necessary to construct a platform for the presentations.

Tableaux and pantomimes could be presented. Some effective tableaux could be worked out on the following themes: The Christ-child in the Manger, The Shepherds, The Wise Men following the Star, The Child Moses in the Bull-rushes.

Appropriate songs should be sung or played during these tableaux.

Bible Plays

For plays running a whole evening "Ruth," "Esther," "The Children of Israel," or some other three-act play could be used. A shorter play would give a chance for greater variety in the program, however. Valuable suggestions could be found in "Dramatized Bible Stories for Young People," by Russell, or "Bible Plays," by Rita Benton.

Games

If desired and practical a few games could be played.

1. *Bible Characters.*—Pin names of Bible characters on the backs of the guests. They must discover whom they represent by the remarks that others make to and about them. As soon as a player discovers his identity he reports to the committee and receives some award.

2. *Living Alphabet.*—See "Animate Alphabet" in Chapter XVI, in "Phunology." Call out Bible names to be spelled. Type—"The name of Abraham's wife. The first side to spell "Sarah" wins a point.

MOONLIGHT PICNIC

The invitations are written on half-moons and read:

> Moonlight night!
> Moonlight bright!
> Picnic? Right!
> Fun? A sight!
>
> We meet at the church at 7 P.M. and go in a body to Centennial Park.

It would add much to the enjoyment of the picnic to

have a committee precede the crowd by an hour or so in order to put up a number of Japanese lanterns. This would give a festive appearance that would do much to put everybody in the right mood for a big time. Some of the games you can play follow:

Squirrel in the Tree

Have the crowd divide into groups of three each. These groups stand about promiscuously. Two of them take hold of hands and form the tree. The third stands between them inside the tree thus formed. Several lost squirrels will be without homes and will stand wherever they desire. The leader blows a whistle and every squirrel must leave its tree immediately to find another. In the general scramble that follows the homeless squirrels try to dodge into a tree. The chances are that several new squirrels will be without homes. The whistle is blown again and there is another wild scramble. The leader should keep the game moving at rapid pace. Every player should be given a chance to be a squirrel. This can be done by the squirrels changing places with the trees. You will find this game a good lively mixer.

Ring

This old game is always popular. The crowd stands in a circle holding a string that runs all the way round. On this string is a ring that is passed along from player to player. A player inside the circle tries to detect what player has the ring. If he tags a player or challenges him and the ring is in either of his hands, that player becomes "It," in turn. Where there is a large circle, it would be well to have several players inside and several rings on the string. To deceive "It" all players keep their hands moving constantly back and forth on the string.

Flying Dutchman

The players stand in a circle by couples. One couple stands outside. This couple runs around, much the same as in "Drop the Handkerchief," and finally taps the hands of one of the couples in the circle. Immediately this couple must run around the circle in opposite direction from the couple that is "It," the idea being to try to get back to position before the other couple occupies it. When the couples meet they must both bow elaborately, the girls courtesying, and the boys going down on one knee.

Chain Tag

Players all stand behind a safety line except one who is "It." When "It" commands "Run," all players must cross the danger territory where "It" holds sway to another safety goal opposite. Players caught by "It" must join hands with him and help catch others. Only outside players in the chain are allowed to tag, and if the chain breaks, all players caught that time are set free. The game continues until every player is caught. It will be necessary to determine an outside boundary line.

Candle Race

The crowd should be divided into two sides and teams should be chosen to represent each side. Six players, for instance, might represent each group. The race would be run in shuttle style, three players from each team being at one end of the course, and three at the other. One player on each team would be provided with a candle. At the signal to go he lights his candle, or another player lights it for him. He must now run to the opposite end of the course and hand the lighted candle to one of his team-mates there. This player starts immediately for the starting point and delivers it to another team-mate. The first team to finish, all six players having run, wins the race. If the candle should go out, the player carrying it must go back, get it lighted, and start over.

Songs

Most everybody enjoys singing. Lead the crowd in singing some of the old favorites that will never die: "My Old Kentucky Home," "The Old Folks At Home," "Carry Me Back to Old Virginny," etc. They will also enjoy "Long, Long, Trail," "Till We Meet Again," "Old McDonald," "John Brown's Baby," "Sweet Ivory Soap," and some of the better class of popular airs.

Other Games

Other games that may be used are "Cat and Rat," "Two-Deep" or "Three-Deep," "Dumb Crambo," and "Jacob and Rachel."

Marshmallow Roast

Have some of the boys make a fire. Each one will provide himself with a long sharp-pointed stick. Marshmallows should be provided in abundance. These are placed on the ends of the sticks and roasted in the flames. This will be a fitting close to your evening of fun.

OUTDOOR BOOK COSTUME PARTY

The invitations could be written in dainty home-made books.

Come dressed to represent
The name of some book,
Or author, or play, or song;
And you will never repent
The time you've thus spent
In mingling with our throng.

Church Lawn. Friday, 8 P. M.

Costumes

The guests are requested to come representing the name of some book, author, play, or song. Each guest is supposed to have one quotation from the book, author, play, or song represented, and must repeat this quotation to any who ask for it. All are provided with cards and pencils and make their guesses as to who or what each guest represents. A prize may also be awarded for the best costume. Some suggestions for costumes:

"Twice-told Tales," chestnuts sewed all over coat or dress; "Black Beauty," black costume with black mask; "Vanity Fair," elaborate dress and constant use of mirror and make-up; "Descent of Man," sash swung from shoulder with letters "M-A-N" printed one letter below the other; "Water Babies," pictures of small fish sewed on dress; "Christmas Carol," copies of carols sewed on coat or dress. Others that will be easy are "The Princess," "The Lamplighter," "Old Black Joe," "If Winter Comes," "Seventeen," "The Three Musketeers," "Longfellow," and "Lightnin'."

Candle Acquaintance

Each one is now given a candle and a slip of paper on which is written the name of some familiar song. At the signal from the leader all candles are lighted, the names of the songs read, and each person begins to sing his song, hunting for the other person in the crowd singing the same song. These two become partners. You can imagine the uproar with all the guests singing at the same time, and singing different songs. It isn't at all harmonious, but it breaks down all stiffness and it's lots of fun.

Charades

Divide the crowd into two sides and let them put on charades representing the name of books, authors, plays, or songs. The guessing group must be told which one of these is being represented.

Pantomime

"Hiawatha" or some other such literary gem could be pantomimed as some one reads it.

Two Writing Stunts

a. Give ten minutes for guests to write down all the celebrated heroines of fiction they can recall. Award prizes for largest list.

b. Give out sheets of paper or tiny home-made books with the names of celebrated heroines written out. Let players identify them by writing opposite each name the title of the book in which her story is told.

FIELD MEET

This should be a big affair between the various churches or schools of the community. Or it might be a combination meet for several small towns.

Plenty of advertising should be done, and arrangements made far enough in advance to allow the churches time to make adequate preparation.

Competent officials should be chosen to handle the Meet. There should be a Registration Committee, and it should be required that the names of all entrants be in their hands by a certain date. You will also need Judges, Announcers (with megaphones), Starter, Clerks-of-Course to attend to measurements and to post scores on a large black-board, Time-keepers, etc.

Events

1. *Tug of War.*
   (*a*) For girls.
   (*b*) For boys.

2. *Fifty Yard Dash* (for Girls).
3. *One Hundred Yard Dash* (for Boys).
4. *Running Broad Jump* (for Boys).
5. *Running High Jump* (for Boys).
6. *Shuttle Relay.*

Seventy-five to 100 yards for the course. Half the runners for each team line up at opposite ends of the course. The first runner for each side runs the distance and touches off his team-mate who stands first on the opposite side of the course. This team-mate, in turn, runs back to the other side and touches off the second runner in line there. This continues until all players have run the course.

7. *Baseball Throwing Contest* (for Distance).
   (*a*) For boys.
   (*b*) For girls.
8. *Fat Men's Race.*
9. *Ladies' Nail Driving Contest.*

Each contestant should be furnished a hammer, a block of wood, and ten nails. The Judges will decide the winner on the basis of speed and skill.

10. *Hobble-Hurdle.*—Tie each contestant's ankles together. Put obstacles five inches high at several places in the course and require that they jump over these as they come to them.

11. *Honeymoon Race.*—Similar to Costume Race. Young man and young woman represent each school. Each couple provided with a suit-case in which are all sorts of ridiculous wearing apparel—kimono, hat, men's slippers, for the girl; and rain-coat, boudoir cap, etc., for the boy. Run to given line, take out apparel, don it, rush back to starting point arm in arm, take off this added apparel, put it back in suit-case, and shut and strap it.

12. *Chariot Race.*—Toy wagon or wheel-barrow. One contestant rides while the other pulls or pushes. Arriving at the opposite side of the course, the rider jumps out,

his team-mate takes his place, and the race is finished at the starting line with the former rider pulling or pushing. It may add some to the interest in this race to have a girl and a boy on each team.

13. *Centipede or Caterpillar Race.*—Five to ten boys represent each group. The team straddles a long pole and races to a given point and back.

14. *Wheelbarrow Race.* (Boys.)—Two boys represent each team. One player supports his body with his hands while the other holds him by the ankles. In this position they race to a given goal.

In these events you will allow five points for first place, three points for second, and one point for third, excepting in the "Tug-of-War," when you will allow ten points for first place, five points for second, and nothing for third. In the "Tug-of-War" it is a good idea to have two ropes available for use so that four teams can pull at once. The winners will pull against one another until you have determined the champion by a process of elimination. Of the last two that pull, one will take first place, and the other second.

Dinner may be served on the grounds and the Meet could well end in a big picnic and jollification.

INDIAN PARTY AND CAMP FIRE

Lee in his "Play in Education" speaks of the "Big Injun" age, but after watching a group of young people at an Indian party we wondered if the "Big Injun" period didn't run through the entire span of life. Given the occasion, a few feathers, and possibly a costume, and the "Big Injun" begins to assert himself, even in the old-timers.

And a camp fire! Well, there's something romantic, mysterious, and fascinating about it. Whether your ancestors were at one time fire-worshippers or not, you find any kind of a fire a tremendous attraction. Haven't you ever had the quiet joy of looking into a grate fire and seeing all sorts of fanciful figures in the licking flames and burning embers? My, what you have missed! And then there was the thrill of a bon-fire! Wasn't it great? Most any kind of fire brings its thrill. We know people who will get up in the middle of the night, dress, and rush madly to a fire, when they hear the fire-bells and see the sky red from some conflagration that may be a mile or so away.

Now link up the "Big Injun" and the "Fire-Worshipper" and we ought to have some party.

Select some beautiful flat location for your party and have the committee set up a few wigwams for decorative purposes. Get enough feathers so that each person can have one to wear. An inch strip of brown cambric will serve as a head-band. The committee should have these on hand. Get some of the boys who know how, to lay your camp fire.

Begin with the following Indian chant, the crowd forming a big circle around the fire:

"Wa kon da de du, Wa pa din, A-toné
Wa kon da de du, Wa pa din, A-toné."

Hands above heads and bend to ground on first line, back to first position on second line.

War Dance

Form two concentric circles, braves inside, squaws outside. At signal braves dance one way, and squaws the other in characteristic Indian style, yelling as they dance.

When the whistle blows all dancing stops and each squaw grabs a brave. They talk for just a few seconds when the whistle blows again. This is the signal for them to start the dance again. A few minutes of this will break up any stiffness and get the crowd in a good mood for an evening of fun.

"Jack's Alive"

Crowd is seated in one big circle. Five or six corks on long sticks have been placed in the fire. When they have started to blaze get several helpers to start them around the circle. As each person handles them he blows on the cork. If the cork shows a spark of red he says, "Humph, Jack heap much alive!" and passes it immediately to the person to his right. This person goes through the same performance, and so it goes around the circle. If a player fails to get a spark, Jack is "heap much dead" and that player must submit to having a mustache, or nose or cheek decoration made on his face by his left-hand neighbor with the burnt cork. All players must enter into the spirit of the game.

An Indian Story

Have the best story-teller you can get tell some Indian legend. It must not be too long.

Squaws' Relay

This is the familiar All-up relay, using Indian clubs. See Phunology, page 184.

Braves' Relay

Use the Obstacle race as suggested on page 184 in "Phunology," or use human obstacles, having one man taking leapfrog position straight, another leapfrog position sideways, another with arms outstretched, another legs stradled, another straight position with arms on side. Contestants must go over first two, under arms of third between legs of four, around fifth man, and back same way.

HORSESHOES OR QUOITS

The regulation distance between pegs in horse shoes is 38½ feet. For girls, this distance will have to be shortened considerably.

The regulation distance for quoits is 30 feet, for senior competition. For the playground this distance may be shortened to 20 feet.

HAY-RIDE AND WATERMELON FESTIVAL

Luscious watermelon and a jolly hay-ride—put these two together and you have a big joyous good time. Ride out into the country or to a park, play a few rollicking games, pull off a few stunts, and wind up with a big watermelon feed.

As a special feature have a watermelon eating contest, making the contestants hold their hands behind them while they eat.

Another special feature could be a Melon Artists' Contest. Each guest, using a pen-knife or other available implement, makes an animal, face, or figure, on his watermelon rind. A prize may be given for the cleverest creation.

TENNIS TOURNAMENT

This may be the grand climax of a season of playing. The schedule of contests should be carefully worked out so as to determine the champions in singles and doubles. Medals or badges may be awarded the winners.

CAMERA HIKE

"You will like
The Camera Hike."

With this slogan you advertise the hike, asking all those who have cameras to bring them along. Pick out a route with many picturesque spots along the way. Let the hikers stop occasionally to take snap-shots. Let it be understood that prizes are to be offered for the best. The committee will divide the pictures into two classes—pictures of nature scenes (landscapes, birds, animals) and pictures of persons. In each of these two classes there will be awards for: (1) The most artistic, (2) The most unique, (3) The most humorous.

All pictures when finished shall be turned in to the committee. It will mount them on cardboard, make its decision, and arrange them artistically around the room for the Camera Party which will follow after the hike by several weeks. Or it may number all pictures and have the crowd vote on the best in the several classes.

Guests at the Camera Party may be asked to turn into the committee baby pictures of themselves. These also should be numbered and guesses made as to the originals of these pictures.

The old Art Gallery guessing game could also be used.

Slides could be made of some of the best of the Hike pictures and they could be thrown on the screen.

QUOITS OR HORSESHOE TOURNAMENT

Like the Tennis Tournament this might be the climax of a season of playing. Quite a good bit of interest could be aroused during the summer in this healthful sport by providing equipment and encouraging every one, including the girls, to participate. The tournament should be well advertised, judges and scorers carefully selected, and all other details carefully planned. Ice-cold lemonade might be served to spectators and contestants.

TRIP AROUND THE WORLD

Tickets may be given out or sold bearing the following instructions:

"WORLD TOUR. Ship leaves the landing at Carson's Lawn, corner Peabody and Dudley Streets, promptly at 7:45 P. M."

Uncle Sam and Miss Columbia greet the guests as they arrive at Carson's Lawn. When the crowd has assembled it is led in the singing of "The Star Spangled Banner" or "America."

Promptly at 7:45, or such time as has been agreed, they depart in automobiles for the home of another member. This is evidently Mexico for there are brilliantly costumed Mexican belles on the lawn, and Mexican men with bright-colored sashes around their waists and large sombreros on their heads. One of the girls plays "La Paloma" as a violin solo. Mexican chili is served from a pretty booth in the center of the lawn by attendants in Mexican costume.

Then, in turn, the touring party visits Scotland, Holland, Japan, and China. Each place is decorated appropriately, Japanese lanterns, perhaps, playing an important part everywhere. Attendants are garbed in the costumes of the particular countries represented. The program and refreshments should also be in keeping. Brief suggestions follow:

Scotland.—Solo or Quartet, "Annie Laurie"; all sing "My Bonnie Lies Over The Ocean"; refreshments, oatmeal cakes.

Holland.—National flag; "Windmill Stunt," three or four orators make speeches, all talking at the same time; refreshments, cheese sandwiches.

Japan.—National flag, numerous open Japanese parasols suspended over lawn, Japanese lanterns; "Fan Ball" (see Phunology, page 187); refreshments, cherry ice.

China.—National flag, numerous dragon panels or curtains about the lawn; "Chinese Hop" (see Phunology, page 164); refreshments, rice cakes and tea.

If the committee desires, it can make this a missionary tour, having large display charts at each place containing facts of interest.

RACES AND GAMES FOR PICNIC AND PARTY

A Wireless Race.—The players line up single file in two or more lines. There is a receiver or judge for each line, who stands on a mark several feet from the head player. A sealed message is given to this player in each line, and the judges also are provided with copies. At the signal to start the seal is broken and the message is read by the player who holds it. He hurriedly whispers it to the next player in line. This player turns immediately and whispers it to the next, and thus it goes until the message has reached the end player. As soon as he gets it he rushes to the receiver for his line and whispers the message to him. The receiver or judge compares the message received with the copy he has. Accuracy as well as speed counts. If two teams tie in accuracy, the race will be decided in favor of the team delivering the message first. Accuracy counts for more than speed, however, and should only one team deliver the message accurately it shall be declared the winner, even though it may be the last in making the delivery. The message should be the same for each team.

Bunny Race.—The runners must assume a stooped position with hands raised bunny fashion. In this position they must make their way to the finish line in short jumps.

Blind Men's Race.—Blindfold the runners and lead them to their positions at the starting point. The runners may have some trouble getting to the finishing line, but that's where the fun comes in.

Chariot or Triangle Race.—Three runners represent each group. They stand with backs to one another and with hands clasped, forming a triangle. In this position they race to a mark and back.

Centipede or Caterpillar Race.—Two or more teams of boys, equal in number, straddle long poles and race to a given point and back. The more boys you can get on the pole the more fun will the race provide.

Crab Race.—The runners go down on all fours and race backwards.

Chinese Hop Race.—This race is a test of skill as well as of speed. Ten sticks are laid down for each contestant at such distances as to easily allow a foot to be placed between them. The runner must hop over all the sticks, stoop and pick up the last stick without touching his raised foot to the ground, and then hop back over the rest of the sticks. He drops stick No. 10 to the ground and goes back for stick No. 9. This he continues until all the sticks have been taken up. If at any time he touches a stick with his foot he must start the race all over again after putting all the sticks back in position. The same penalty may be imposed for touching the raised foot to the ground, though in the case of inexperienced players it may be allowable to touch the foot to the ground before each start. This race may also be run as a relay, with ten runners for each side. In this case the starting line would be about six feet from the first stick.

Dizzy Izzy.—This race is one of the most amusing of all

races. Each contestant is furnished with a stick or cane about as long as the ordinary umbrella. Placing the end of the stick firmly to the ground, he must put both hands on the top and rest his head on his hands. Then with eyes open he must go around the stick four times without lifting it from the ground or taking his head from the position first taken. In the case of younger boys, it may be advisable to require that they turn around as many as seven times. After making the required number of turns, the runner must race to and around a tree, pole, chair, or whatever has been designated, and return to the starting point. This race is exceptionally effective as a relay. In this case the two teams would line up single file behind the starting line, and each man, in turn, would begin his turning around the stick as his team-mate returns and hands it to him. It would be well to have a starter for each stick to count the turns for each runner so that no contestant shall unwittingly take advantage of his opponents by not making the required number.

Duck or Ankle Race.—Each runner must take hold of his ankles, and holding this position, race to the finish line.

Dog Race.—The contestants must race forward on all fours, galloping dog-fashion.

Derby Jig.—The contestants must stoop and clasp hands around their knees. In this position they must race to the goal.

Horse Race.—Two boys for each team. They race to a given point, each boy mounted on his team-mate's back. At the goal line the rider dismounts and he becomes the horse. Thus the return is made.

"AS YOU WERE!"

Here is a good mixing game that will probably thaw out your crowd if the commands are given snappily.

Have the girls and boys line up single file in different rooms. Let them now march out into the main room, the two lines meeting and thus matching partners. The partners now form a circle, boys on the outside. (A simple expedient for a crowd where the boys and girls are not present in equal numbers is the use of a white handkerchief tied about the arm to make the proper balance. Thus a girl with a white handkerchief around her arm becomes a boy for the purposes of the game.)

The leader now takes the center of the circle and calls the command, "March!" The couples circle about him. Next he shouts, "Girls outside, boys inside!" Then, "Girls in front of boys!" Then, "Halt, and face partners!" Then, "The grand right and left!" In this the couples clasp right hands and pass to each other's right. Then with the next partner they clasp left hands and pass to the left. They continue to alternate in this way, thus winding in and out, the girls going in one direction and the boys in the other, until the leader shouts, "As you were!" when each person must find his first partner and assume the first position of the game. In this scramble the leader endeavors to get a partner. The player left out is "It."

In a large crowd two leaders may be used, one being a boy and the other a girl.

[NOTE.—If the players have never before tried the grand right and left, it would be best to explain it clearly before the game starts, staging a demonstration with a few players.]

HUNT THE SLIPPER

Players form in a circle with one player, who is "It," in the center. All players face center with hands behind them. Some one in the circle has a slipper in his hands, which he passes to one of his neighbors. At any time he desires, "It" may challenge any player to show both hands. If the slipper happens to be in the called player's possession he becomes "It" in turn, and the game continues. It is allowable for any player to hit "It" in the back with the slipper. The slipper is then tossed back to some player in the circle, and after "It" counts ten the game is on again.

STATUE RACE

Contestants line up at one side of the room. A leader stands in front of them. When he turns his back and walks from them they may walk, not run, as rapidly as it is possible. Immediately he whirls about facing them they must stop, holding the position in which they happen to be at the moment. Players not observing this rule must go back to the starting point and begin all over. To make the game interesting the leader must turn at the most unexpected moments. This he continues to do until the winner of the race has crossed the line.

SHOPPING

Here's a game that can be used either indoors or outdoors with good results. Group the players by couples around four tables. Let one of the tables be decorated with a sign that reads "Dry goods," another "Drugs," another "Groceries," and the fourth "Books and Stationery." On each table have a pile of letters turned face down. One player at a time at each table turns up a letter, and the first player at that table to call out some article that may be bought in this particular shop gets the letter. Thus some one at the "Dry goods" table turns up the letter "C," and immediately some player calls out "Calico." At the end of the agreed time the shoppers all move to another table in such order that each group will make the round of shops. At the close of the shopping round the couple with the largest number of letters may be awarded some sort of prize. This game may be played in progressive fashion. In this case the high couple at each table would move up to another table.

JUMP THE SHOT

The players form a big circle with one player in the center. This player has a long heavy string, on the end of which is tied a bean bag or a small bag of sand. A long fishing pole would serve even better. He whirls this around close to the ground, and the players in the circle must avoid being hit by jumping over it as it reaches them. When a player is hit he must immediately drop out of the circle. The last player in the circle may be center man for the next game.

POOR LITTLE PUSSY CAT (SIDES)

Line up the players in two sides facing one another. Side No. 1 sends its first player over to the first player on Side No. 2. He must kneel before No. 2 and say "Meow" three times. Each time No. 2 must pat him on the head and say solemnly: "Poor little pussy cat." If No. 2 should smile or laugh, he must drop out of line. The next player from side No. 2 now goes over and kneels to the player on No. 1 who is opposite him, going through the same performance. At the close the side with the most players in line is declared winner.

A variation of this plan would be to have all the players

of one side kneel to the other at one time. The other side would then take its turn in trying to disturb the solemnity of its opponents.

FISH NET

The players form in two lines. Boundary lines are determined so that the distance between the safety goals is about the width of a ordinary gymnasium. For thirty players the length of the field would be just about the length of a gymnasium. For a larger group the field would have to be lengthened. One group of players stands behind the safety goal on one side. The other group stands in the middle of the space between the two lines, all players clasping hands. Its captain shouts "Fish net!" and sweeps toward the safety goal behind which the other side stands trying to catch as many players in the net as is possible. Only end players can tag an opponent, and thus players may escape by dodging around the fish net or by ducking under the arms of those forming it, a means that the net players may prevent by blocking the runner until one of the end players can tag him. When a player reaches the safety zone on the other side he is free for the time being. Each player caught in the net must drop out. If the net is broken by any of the players unclasping hands, all fish caught in that sweep are released. After five sweeps or such a number as may be decided by mutual agreement, the sides change places. The side catching the most fish is declared winner.

SPELL-DOWN

The group is divided into two equal sides which face one another. The game may be played in two ways:

1. The head player on one side begins a word giving

the first letter. The opposite player on the other side adds a letter. Then it goes back to the second player on the first side, and so on until somebody finishes a word. If a word is finished the player is out. For instance the first player says "S." The opposite player immediately says "O," and is out for finishing the word "so." It makes no difference what word the player has in mind. If he finishes a word he is out.

If a player doubts that his opponent is really spelling a word and it is his time to add a letter, he may challenge by saying "I challenge you." The player must then tell what word he has in mind. If he cannot answer he is out. If he does answer correctly, the challenger is out.

The idea of the game is to see which side can have players standing longest.

2. In this case the players have to spell a word beginning with the last letter of the word the opponent has just spelled. Thus player No. 1 on the "Blues" spells "thread." Number 1 on the "Reds" immediately begins with "drone." The next player on the "Blues" begins a word with "E," and so on. No repetitions are allowed, and a player must spell his word before the referee can count "ten." A player counted out, drops out of line.